Open Data and the Know

T0220896

Open Data and the Knowledge Society

Bridgette Wessels, Rachel L. Finn,
Kush Wadhwa and Thordis Sveinsdottir

Amsterdam University Press

Cover design: Coördesign, Leiden
Lay-out: Crius Group, Hulshout

Amsterdam University Press English-language titles are distributed in the US and Canada by
the University of Chicago Press.

ISBN   978 94 6298 018 1
e-ISBN   978 90 4852 936 0
DOI   10.5117/9789462980181
NUR   983

Printed and bound by CPI Group (UK) Ltd, Croydon, CR0 4YY

Contents

Acknowledgements

The authors would like to acknowledge the crucial contributions of the contributors and project partners in the *Policy RECommendations for Open access to research Data in Europe* (RECODE) project. The following individuals' research and thought leadership contributed to overarching themes within the project:

- Lorenzo Bigagli and Stefano Nativi, from the National Research Council of Italy, who contributed a chapter to the book.
- Peter Linde from the Blekinge Institute of Technology, Sweden.
- Merel Noorman, who contributed a chapter to the book, and Sally Wyatt from the Royal Netherlands Academy of Arts and Sciences, the Netherlands.
- Susan Reilly from LIBER, the Netherlands.
- Rod Smallwood, Mark J. Taylor and Lada Price, from the University of Sheffield, UK.
- Jeroen Sondervan from the Amsterdam University Press, the Netherlands.
- Victoria Tsoukala, Marina Angelaki and Vasso Kalaitzi from the National Documentation Centre, Greece.

These individuals represented their respective organisations in the highly collaborative RECODE project, and this book has emerged from their collaboration. The project was funded by the European Commission (Grant number 321463 Programme: Seventh Framework Programme for Science in Society), under the leadership of Daniel Spichtinger (EC Project Officer).

An integral part of this research was the examination of real-world cases involving the use of open research data. We thank all of the case study organisations – the Physics Department at the University of Sheffield, the European Commission funded Markers for emphysema versus airway disease in COPD (EVA) project, the University of Auckland Bioengineering Institute, the Group on Earth Observation System of Systems (GEOSS) and the European Commission's Joint Research Centre (JRC) as well as the Alexandria Archive Institute – for their valuable insights and for giving their time to the project. We would also like to thank the RECODE Advisory Board for their important contributions, including Toby Burrows, Massimo Craglia, Jerome Reichman and Shaun Topham. In addition, we are grateful to the many participants in the RECODE research who attended and contributed to workshops and who granted our researchers interviews.

Finally, many thanks to Helen Rana for her excellent proof-reading and commenting on the text and for the index, to the team at Amsterdam University Press, and to the reviewer whose comments greatly improved the manuscript.

List of acronyms

CSOs	Civil Society Organisations
DCC	Digital Curation Centre
DMP	Data management plan
DPC	Data publishing charge
EC	European Commission
EDPS	European Data Protection Supervisor
G8	Group of Eight (highly-industrialised countries)
GEOSS	Group on Earth Observation System of Systems
GIS	Geographic information system
ICT	Information and communication technologies
IGOs	Intergovernmental organisations
IoT	Internet of Things
IPR	Intellectual Property Rights
ODF	Open Data Foundation
ODI	Open Data Institute
OECD	The Organisation for Economic Co-operation and Development
OGD	Open Government Data
OGG	Open Government Group
OKF	Open Knowledge Foundation
OKFN	Open Knowledge Foundation Network
OKI	Open Knowledge International
PI	Persistent identifier
PSI	Public Sector Information
RECODE	Policy Recommendations on Open Access to Research Data in Europe
SME	Small- and medium enterprises
W3C	World Wide Web Consortium
WIPO	World Intellectual Property Organisation
WWW	World Wide Web
WWWF	World Wide Web Foundation

1. Introduction

The idea of a knowledge society has been advanced over the last two decades, but the transition to such a society has not yet been realised in reality. Discussions around a knowledge society have largely focused on a knowledge economy and information society, rather than a mobilisation to a knowledge society. These debates have, however, taken place prior to the rise of open data and big data and the ensuing development of an open data movement. This book considers the role of the open data movement in fostering transformation to a knowledge society. The characteristics of the open data movement include the strong conviction of the value of open data for society, attention to the institutional aspects of making data open in an inclusive way and a practical focus on the technological infrastructure that is key to enabling a knowledge society. At the heart of any mobilisation is an emerging open data ecosystem and new ways of producing and using data – whether 'born digital' data, digitised data or big data – and how that data, when made openly available, can be used in a well-informed and beneficial way by societal actors.

The book examines how the idea of open data has been taken up by civil society actors and the policymaking community. It considers whether these actors' activities constitute a social movement that is seeking to mobilise open data and, significantly, whether that work is fostering a transition from an information society based on a knowledge economy into a knowledge society. In order to assess this broad question, it is necessary to explore some key areas of work that are needed to facilitate open data. These include changing institutional frameworks around data, generating data formats that can be made open, generating technical infrastructure and governance models, and addressing research practices and legal and ethical concerns in making data open. To mobilise each of these areas, change is required in the way that each works, along with the creation of new processes and practices. Further, and beyond change in each area, each aspect of change has to interact and link with the other, so that an holistic open data environment is developed. Even though these aspects are important in the mobilisation of open data, social participation in the mobilisation of knowledge society is also needed for such a transformation to occur. Considering participation in the transformation to a knowledge society and participation in a knowledge society raises questions about the position of science in society and the way in which citizens, businesses and civil society actors can participate by using open data. Only then, when the aspects of an open data environment come together and societal actors can use open data in a socially-defined way, can we say that there is a transformation to a knowledge society.

To assess the role of open data in society and in any transformations to a knowledge society, it is necessary to define what the information society, knowledge economy and knowledge society. In this book, we use *information society* to refer to societies in which information is a central feature in production, innovation and consumption, and which is organised via digital networks. This type of society often has a strong service sector and its economy is driven by knowledge garnered from flows of information. A *knowledge economy* is the economic structure of an information society, because the economy is driven by knowledge that is created from information. Further, this economy is characterised by rapid and continuous innovation, and is global in scope. It draws on an educated workforce within commercial and university research centres that specialise in handling data and information to remain globally competitive in a dynamic and fast-paced global economy. The idea of an information society and its attendant knowledge economy is based on a model where information is not an open commodity and, hence, innovation and growth are managed through private investment and outsourced university spin-outs. This differs from the notion of a *knowledge society*, although there is debate about the precise definition of this. In general terms, a knowledge society distinguishes itself from an information society and knowledge economy because it sees information and knowledge as open to all. Its central value is openness, which means that data, information and knowledge are seen as a 'commons' or shared asset in society. This has the potential to allow any member of society to use data to engage and participate in economic, social, political and cultural projects. Thus, a transformation to a knowledge society is radical in that it seeks to foster open social relations amongst people.

The main argument of this book is that the combination of a proliferation of data and the open data movement are significant features in the possibility of generating and mobilising a knowledge society. A key aspect of mobilising data within a knowledge society framework is the actions of a network of actors who together generate an open data movement, which also interacts with a range of public and private institutions and high levels of digital and digitised data. One factor in the mobilisation of knowledge society is how data can be made openly available and then utilised within wider society. It is envisaged that open data has the potential to foster economic growth and social well-being. However, for this potential to be realised, the data will have to be of high quality and able to be reused and shared across society. The book focuses on how the open data movement is interacting with three features that are shaping a new data environment: (1) the emergent characteristics of data; (2) a new socio-technical data ecosystem; and (3) a new configuration of institutions that are shaping and mobilising data across a data ecosystem and wider society, along with the development of interpretive communities.

RECODE

The conclusions of and information within this book are based largely on the empirical work conducted within a European Commission funded project called Policy Recommendations on Open Access to Research Data in Europe (RECODE). The primary objective of RECODE was to reduce fragmentation within the open access to research data ecosystem by providing evidence-based and overarching policy recommendations based on good practice. In order to achieve this, RECODE was based around four grand challenges and five disciplinary case studies. The grand challenges included an in-depth, empirical investigation of (1) stakeholder values and inter-relationships; (2) technological barriers; (3) legal and ethical issues; and (4) institutional and policy issues. The five case studies were comprised of:

- **Particle physics and particle astrophysics** – Experiments associated with particle physics often produce extremely large volumes of data. For example, the Large Hadron Collider (LHC) at CERN produces about 15 petabytes of data each year, and requires a custom-made computing grid to collect, analyse and store all of the data produced. As part of the RECODE project, the physics department at the University of Sheffield was used to identify and examine any legal and ethical issues involved in collecting, disseminating, storing and processing large quantities of numerical data from experiments related to particle physics. Central to this examination was the fact that the expertise and resources necessary for storing and processing the data are only available to established experts in the field and/or very large consortia.

- Health and clinical research – The case study focused on the ethical issues surrounding data sharing and open data as well as data security of highly sensitive human data. RECODE used the European Commission-funded Markers for emphysema versus airway disease in COPD (EVA)[1] project as

---

1   See http://cordis.europa.eu/project/rcn/87739_en.html for more information.

a starting point to examine the legal and ethical issues associated with giving open access to health research data. This meant interviewing project experts as well as associated experts in clinical, health and biological data.

- **Bioengineering** – The bioengineering case study focused on the relationship between data sets and complex computational models, with a specific focus on the use or processing of data from human subjects. The starting point for the case study was the University of Auckland's Bioengineering Institute (http://www.abi.auckland.ac.nz/en.html), and it included additional experts in the Virtual Physiological Human (VPH) community involved in ontology development, standards for model description and curation of model repositories.

- **Environmental sciences** – The environmental sciences case study focused on the Group on Earth Observation System of Systems (GEOSS) (Group on Earth Observations, 2014) and the RECODE investigation, which is primarily situated within the European Commission's Joint Research Centre (JRC). The GEOSS group uses existing systems and applications for geographic monitoring, including taking observations around drought, forestry, biodiversity and other earth science domains, which include contributions from multiple actors in many countries around the world. In addition to providing interoperable access to data, GEOSS also seeks to develop an advanced operating capacity that provides access to analytical models, which scientists from different disciples can use to make the data more understandable.

- **Archaeology** – The archaeology case study focused on 'Open Context' (opencontext.org/), a digital repository administered by the Alexandria Archive Institute (https://alexandriaarchive.org), a not-for-profit organisation[2] in the US. Open Context is a free, open access resource that enables the electronic publication of diverse types of research data sets from archaeology and related disciplines. In addition to providing data, it also offers useful information regarding attitudes, practices and policies within the archaeology research ecosystem, along with technical information about depositing, accessing and preserving archaeological data.

Despite the specificity of these case study descriptions, as the RECODE project developed, it became clear that the issues identified in each case

---

2   Open context is financially supported by The William and Flora Hewlett Foundation, The National Endowment for the Humanities and The Institute of Museum and Library Services.

study should be more broadly considered, extending the research to stakeholders within and outside of each specific study. Therefore, for example, some of the archaeology case study quotes presented in the chapters that follow are not only from participants directly involved in the specific case study organisation, but also from people involved in a range of other organisations within the open access to an archaeological data ecosystem. Thus, they should be read as academic disciplinary case studies, rather than organisational case studies. Nevertheless, the grand challenges and case studies created a matrix where each grand challenge was examined in each discipline. These case studies provided an interdisciplinary grounding, helping to maintain an awareness of discipline-specific issues and practices as well as providing insight into the grand challenges.

The specific RECODE methodology consisted of a three-step process: an extensive review of the literature, interviews with stakeholders within the disciplinary case studies and stakeholder validation workshops. The literature reviewed consisted of policy literature (e.g. national, European and international policy), practice literature (e.g. publication, data management and ethical protocols), grey literature (e.g. manifestos, white papers and blog posts from open access organisations/visionaries), and academic literature. In total, the project conducted 65 semi-structured interviews with academics, researchers, policymakers, data centre staff, legal experts, scientific publishers and other experts working within the field of open access to research data. Findings from the literature review and case studies were then further validated in five stakeholder workshops, which, in total, counted 168 workshop participants from 35 countries. The workshop attendees came from different stakeholder groups, e.g. policymakers, data managers, researchers, academics, librarians and publishers. The validation events offered the opportunity to discuss and debate the findings of RECODE and test their relevance and applicability in a broader context.

RECODE was an original opportunity to examine the interrelationship between a particular sphere of the larger open access movement and the impact of that movement on both stakeholders within it and the larger scientific and research culture. It is the first study to take the open access movement itself as an object of investigation. Thus, it provides empirical evidence about the ways in which data is being shaped by and shaping research culture, the institutional, technical and social ecosystems that are emerging within this open data movement and the ways in which institutions have adapted to this emerging landscape.

The book

This book is a jointly authored book that is based on the research in the RE-CODE project. Bridgette Wessels is the lead author and she wrote Chapters One, Two, Three, Four and Ten as well as overseeing and commenting on the work of the other authors. Rachel Finn wrote Chapter Eight, co-wrote Chapter Nine and read and commented on the whole book. Merel Noorman wrote Chapter Five, Thordis Sveinsdottir wrote Chapter Six, Lorenzo Bigagli and Stefano Naviti wrote Chapter Seven, and Kush Wadhwa co-wrote Chapter Nine.

In order to explore the issues of open data discussed above, the book is structured in the following way. Chapter Two, 'Defining a Knowledge Society', reviews the debates about the meaning of a knowledge society in relation to discussions around an information society. It argues that the way in which the open data movement is driving for data to be openly available is a key feature of the emergence of a knowledge society. There are, however, barriers and risks in making data open, which are discussed in the chapters that follow. The term 'knowledge society' was first coined by Peter Drucker in 1969, but it was not developed further until the mid- to late 1990s, when scholars such as Robin Mansell (1998) and Nico Stehr (1994) explored the idea further. Work by Mansell and Stehr points out that debates about an information society cannot be separated from considerations about a knowledge society. This is because the notions of an information society rest, to some degree, on commercial and economic networks of society that are technologically supported, whereas the concept of a knowledge society encompasses other dimensions, such as ethical and political concerns within social life. Stehr (1994, 2004, 2012) argues that the development of a knowledge society is a gradual process that is not deliberately triggered by human design but, instead, is shaped by the way that new technologies, new data fields, new needs, and new imaginations interact and configure to produce new possibilities and innovations. Stehr (1994) defines knowledge as a capacity for action, which, he argues, has multifaceted implications. In general terms, knowledge is different from information, in that it requires cultural interpretation to create it. In summary, UNESCO makes some ethical and normative suggestions within a development paradigm by asserting that, to 'remain human and liveable, knowledge societies will have to be societies of shared knowledge' (UNESCO 2005). It is thus arguing for an open approach to knowledge, and data is very much part of this dynamic. We conclude this chapter by noting that, although there are various definitions of knowledge society or societies, there is a strong call from regional to global actors for policy for 'activating knowledge' (Soete 1997).

The main argument of Chapter Three, 'Visions of Open Data', is that the value of data is realised through its own characteristics as well as by the way it can be used in specific contexts. It is difficult to define data in a way that is sufficiently precise, yet broad enough to capture the richness and diversity of data. 'Data' as a concept can be viewed as the lowest level of abstraction, from which information and then knowledge are derived. In general terms, data is a set of values of qualitative or quantitative variables. The presence of data, as something already found, or something created through research processes, or as a by-product of social media is seen to have value, either in itself or in its reuse. The chapter considers the way that definitions of open data have been developed by actors in civil society. In particular, it notes how some civil society actors' visions of open data link with ideas about open knowledge and an open knowledge society. In the context of civil society organisations that act as advocates for open data, the focus is on the characteristics of open knowledge and what its context of use could be. Another vision of open data can be found at the government level. In this context, there are a set of principles and guidelines about open data as well as visions for its use. Another area that is developing visions of the use of open data is academia, where the focus is on open access to research data and how that might benefit the academic and scientific communities. In the area of big data, the proliferation of open data carries significant potential for the construction of big data sets; however, the integration of these data resources has yet to be adequately realised to enable this transition.

Chapter Four, 'Mobilising Open Data', addresses how open data is being adopted in society. As the previous chapters show, the position of scientific knowledge in wider social and economic life has changed in late modernity. They also show that data and open data are being discussed in civil society and by governments in ways that focus on the possible social benefits of open data. These two areas – the changing role of knowledge in society and the possible benefits of open data – should be viewed in relation to each other, because the aspirations for open data are often couched within understandings of the role that knowledge plays in society. Furthermore, the possibility of open data combined with changing senses of the position of knowledge in society are utilised in various visions of a more knowledgeable society. Within these discussions, there is a recognition of the potential benefits to society, as well as the possible threats and risks of open data. An overarching theme in these discourses is that of 'open' – both in terms of open data and open society. The chapter brings together these discussions by showing how the main theme of openness in open data is a key driver of change, concluding that there is a strong conviction by those in the open data movement that open data has the potential to be valuable for society, in both general and specific terms. The consensus about the value of open data is applied to a wide range of social and economic areas, such as open government, development and human rights, innovation and commerce. However, the realisation of that ambition is complex and requires technological, institutional, legal and cultural change in a social transformation to a knowledge society.

Chapters Five, Six, Seven and Eight are all based upon findings from RECODE, where empirical information from the project is used as a platform from which to consider the interrelationships between providing open access to research data and progressing towards a knowledge society. Chapter Five, 'Institutions in the Data Ecosystem', discusses the importance of institutions in socio-technical change and in their role as curators of data in the mobilisation of a knowledge society. The chapter discusses the role that these play in the changing data environment, and refers to diverse institutions including research councils and institutes, foundations, policymakers, advocacy groups, Civil Society Organisations (CSOs), universities, scholarly societies, intergovernmental organisations (IGOs), standards organisations, service providers, data centres, information aggregators, libraries and archives, publishers, professional associations, scholarly societies, public sector data collectors, and private sector big data collectors. These institutions form part of an emerging open data ecosystem and are grouped in this chapter by their key functions, which include funding, creating data, creating data repositories, curating data, accessing data, and using and disseminating data. The chapter also addresses some of the challenges that such institutions face. In particular, it explores the challenges involved in navigating between the competing interests of heterogeneous stakeholders, entrenched institutional cultures and wide-ranging and, sometimes, conflicting ideas about open data. It considers the opportunities for institutions to contribute to an open data ecosystem that will benefit the knowledge society.

Chapter Six, 'Scientific Disciplines, Scientific Practice and Making Research Data Open', argues that the move to openness requires a change in research practices and the ways in which data is gathered, stored and analysed. It also argues that scientific disciplines face different barriers in their move towards open access to research data, since the research process requires procedures to ensure the generation of data that can be openly available, accessible, and reusable. The chapter draws on qualitative research in five scientific disciplines: archaeology, bioengineering, environmental sciences, health and clinical research and particle physics. It demonstrates how their contribution to knowledge generation is based on different scientific practices, and details how they are having to adapt in order to participate in the move towards open access research data. The chapter also highlights the increasing and emergent complexity of contemporary scientific practice with respect to interdisciplinary research, sophisticated technology (e.g. simulations), international collaborations and vast amounts of data, discussing how these may complicate the process of research and, consequently, the production, analysis and storage of data. The chapter considers how the move to openness in science is supported by the notion of the knowledge society, where knowledge is no longer limited to a small, exclusive group, but is seen as a public good. Science plays an important role in society, because the production and advancement of knowledge are among its key aims. Open access to research data is one aspect of transferring knowledge and gaining the ability to bring new knowledge closer to the public. In order for this to happen, disciplines will need to consider the role of data in their research practices and decide how it can be made reusable and accessible. This chapter considers the barriers and opportunities that exist within different scientific disciplines.

Chapter Seven, 'Environmental Data, Technical and Governance Issues', introduces some of the specific features of mobilising open data, by focusing on one context in which this is already happening – the geospatial data sector, including environmental data and earth sciences. This case study shows how the use of open data to support the challenges facing the world in terms of global environmental challenges is supported by scientists, governments, policymakers and activists. This generalised sense of consensus has helped stakeholders to mobilise some levels of open data within its broad community. In addition, efforts to strengthen the political cohesion of geographical regions (e.g. the EU), to digitise public administration, to better understand and mitigate global-scale phenomena (e.g. climate change), or the growing interest in space programmes, are all greatly contributing to the momentum of the open data movement in the geospatial sector. The chapter elaborates on the geospatial data ecosystem and the way that its stakeholders are addressing technological issues such as interoperability at the infrastructural as well as the semantic level. The chapter also considers the issue of governance, which is recognised as one of the most important aspects of developing open access to geospatial data. This requires mutually-agreed policies on the exchange, sharing, access and use of interoperable data and services across various levels of public authority and different sectors of society, at a global level.

Chapter Eight, 'Navigating Legal and Ethical Frameworks', address the issues of ethical, legal and regulatory frameworks in the sciences and humanities for mobilising open data. In many contexts, ethical, legal and social issues have been construed as a barrier or challenge to providing open access to data, especially data that raises intellectual property considerations or data relating to people that could infringe people's personal privacy (particularly identifiable individuals). However, alongside the need to meet legal obligations and ethical standards around research and data collection, some stakeholders are being strongly encouraged to enable a realisation of the knowledge society, either through making as much of their data as possible open, or by exploiting their data to enable innovation. This is being advocated, in particular, by policymakers, funders and some civil society organisations within the open data movement. Researchers, data centres and institutions emerge as key stakeholders in relation to these (sometimes) competing demands, and these groups are often leveraging existing infrastructures or devising new solutions to tackle these issues simultaneously. This chapter examines the interplay between ethical, legal and regulatory frameworks in the provision of open access to research data in order to enable the knowledge society. It addresses the intersecting and, sometimes, competing governance structures being navigated by researchers, institutions and data centres. At the governmental level, these may be legal or legislative obligations, such as privacy, data protection and intellectual property, which may be mandated by national or supranational (e.g. European) levels of government. The chapter asserts that understanding legal and ethical obligations as challenges or barriers can bring about that very effect. Strong legal protections and ethical practice will foster trust in data practices, institutions and governance structures, which will encourage stakeholders to provide data and to open and share that data. Constructing solutions to the legal and ethical issues will therefore support efforts to integrate open data into the knowledge society.

Chapter Nine, 'Big Data, Open Data and the Commercial Sector', examines opportunities for innovation through the intersections between big data and open data. It focuses on policymakers' expectations that big data and the increasing availability of external data resources would result in significant opportunities for innovation in Europe, the US and globally. While large technology companies in the US have dominated the big data ecosystem thus far, policymakers expect that small- and medium enterprises (SMEs) should also be key beneficiaries of this potential for innovation. Using information from the Open Data 500 lists, this section examines the extent to which SMEs have been able to capitalise on this opportunity for innovation. It argues that the fruits of the big data evolution are situated within a complex innovation space that initially produces benefits for large enterprises, which have significant capacity for investment in infrastructure and capabilities. These benefits slowly expand to permeate into small actors directly within the large company's ecosystem, then onto actors outside the bounded ecosystem, in wider society. The chapter also examines the extent to which policymakers' and civil society organisations' advocacy for open data might introduce additional complexity into this innovation space, by prioritising the openness of data in ways that might make it difficult for SMEs to protect the sustainability of their innovations. Finally, the discussion concludes with a consideration of the uneven distribution of big data innovation globally. Rather than expressing concern about a lack of visible innovation in Europe in comparison to the US, the chapter argues that Europe's strong protections for privacy and intellectual property rights themselves provide an opportunity for innovation. Thus, instead of trying to emulate the US, Europe should be investing in creating an innovation space that reflects and reinforces European values, particularly those about responsible innovation, as this will ultimately support some elements of a knowledge society.

Chapter Ten, the conclusion, argues that the vision sought by the open data movement is a key feature of the way that social participation and innovation is being considered by policymakers and industry as well as by the civic society stakeholders and institutions involved in the production of knowledge. The open data movement is interacting with other key features discussed in the book, which are: (1) the emergent characteristics of data; (2) a new socio-technical data ecosystem; and (3) a new configuration of institutions that are shaping and mobilising data across a data ecosystem and wider society, along with the development of interpretive communities.

The development of a new data ecosystem is currently in its infancy, so several issues need to be addressed, such as governance, interoperability, data curation, licensing and ethical issues. Furthermore, institutions and organisations in both the public and private sectors are reconsidering how they value data and how they might share and make that data open in ways that could benefit society. The open data advocates have come together to form a movement as a network of networks and, in this form, constitute a key actor in fostering open data. There will, however, need to be a shift in social imagination in terms of how to use data, as Stehr argues, as well as further development of the data environment and its interpretive communities in order to mobilise a knowledge society. Nonetheless, the open data movement has moved society some way towards being able to provide an important element in the mobilisation and transformation from an information society to a knowledge society.

2. Defining a 'knowledge society'

Introduction

To address what 'knowledge society' refers to means understanding how data is embedded in society and in what ways we can view society as a learning phenomenon. Society is, in many ways, shaped by the way it learns – how it can organise ways to produce goods and services and to consume those goods and services. This process of production and consumption requires knowledge and cultural interpretation and, thus, social life is defined through production, consumption and interpretation. There are different domains of knowledge, some of which are closer to production and consumption while others are more esoteric. The meaning of knowledge is discussed further in the next chapter. Nonetheless, knowledge is created socially and, over time, the production and consumption of knowledge has changed. This chapter discusses the ways in which knowledge has been produced historically and how it is produced in contemporary society.

The specific social change in question is the move from an information society based on a knowledge economy to one based on a knowledge society. There are a range of definitions of the term 'knowledge society', but, broadly speaking, a knowledge society is one that generates, processes, shares and makes knowledge that may be used to improve the human condition available to all its members (Castelfranchi 2007). Castelfranchi (*Ibid.*) asserts that a knowledge society differs from an information society, because it seeks to transform data into resources that allow society to take effective action towards creating a genuinely participative society where everyone can benefit from access to knowledge and contribute to knowledge. This differs from an information society, in which information is the key commodity in production, consumption and innovation. An information society's economy – a knowledge economy – uses information to create knowledge to fuel innovation and economic growth. This means that an information society circulates information within selected economic, political and social networks and has a more limited social agenda of inclusion (Wessels 2010). Therefore, assessing what changes are required to transform into a knowledge society, and what role data might have in that, requires understanding how society organises the production and distribution of knowledge.

Although knowledge is produced in many areas of social life, since early modernity one of the main areas of the production of knowledge is science. The institution of science has shaped, and continues to shape, how formal knowledge is understood. The role and position of science has changed over time, and they may well continue to change in any possible transformations into a knowledge society. Change in the role and position of science is significant in two main areas: first, the ways in which science defines knowledge and produces data; and second, how science and scientific knowledge relate to other areas of society. Together, these two points combine in terms of understanding how formal scientific knowledge is produced and shared across the social relations of society. The characteristics of the social relations of society also shape the values that underpin knowledge and determine how it should be used. To explore how one can start define knowledge, this chapter first discusses data within society, before outlining society as a social and human product. It then discusses science, knowledge production and society in general terms, then goes on to consider the position of knowledge production and distribution in post-industrial and information societies. Next, the chapter discusses the conceptualisation of information society, knowledge economy and knowledge society. It concludes by emphasising that, even though formal knowledge has become more integrated into society, there remains a limited openness to data.

Data in society

To consider how a society might be transformed from an information society into a knowledge society means understanding how data sits within that society. This is because the production and use of data is shaped by a range of social relations within sectors and across sectors of society that include the commercial and public sectors as well as scholarly research.

The term 'data' is widely used amongst academics, researchers, professionals in the public, private and third sectors as well as by the general public. Data, information and knowledge are often considered in relation to each other. In general terms, data is collected and analysed to create information suitable for use in decision-making, while knowledge is developed from extensive experience gained from dealing with information on a subject (Beynon-Davies 2002). Data is pervasive and is used in all aspects of social life. It is collected, coded, interpreted and used across a range of social practices, which are shaped by the production and consumption patterns of particular social contexts and sectors. Therefore, although data, information and knowledge are broad abstract terms, they also have distinctive characteristics resulting from their respective collection and processing methods as well as the uses envisaged for them.

It is important to understand data in a social context, because the specific characteristics of data are shaped by their contexts of production and consumption. One area of society that has historically had a role in creating data is science. The role of science in society and its particular characteristics create data and assess the validity and value of particular data. Although data can be viewed as a general category, it is also specific, and different data have distinctive characteristics. As science develops and changes over time, the meaning and relevance of data also changes. Of course, science is not the only source of data, but scientific data has a particular value, appreciation and use within scholarship and, in some instances, in wider social life as well.

One way to consider data in society is to examine the way that society is organised and the sectors of its organisation, including the role of science as an institution. The characteristics of particular institutions and sectors and the relations between them are constituted within particular types of society. Definitions of society are usually based on their relations of production, types of political systems and their respective social and cultural orders. The precise configuration of these dimensions produces distinctive types of society, such as agrarian, industrial or information society (Wessels 2014). The characteristics of data and knowledge vary in the context of these different societies, while data and knowledge are both shaped by the social relations of society. The different understandings of data and the character of the data itself are generated within society and the way in which society organises and orders its material and symbolic resources. By looking at society and social relations in this way, one can appreciate how data is embedded within social relations including science, and how these social relations create and shape the data production and use.

Society as a social and human product: Learning, knowledge and institutions

The precise definition of 'society' is highly debated in academic sociology. However, in broad terms, society refers to the way in which humans come together to construct ways of organising life – and Berger and Luckmann's (1967) contention that society is a human product illustrates this point well. Berger and Luckmann (*Ibid.*) assert that human self-production is 'always, and of necessity, a social enterprise' (1967, p. 51). They continue by

arguing that ongoing human production is ensured through the development of social order, which is created through human action. The ordering
of activities in social life is partly achieved through habitualisation, which
is any action that is repeated enough to become a pattern, which can then
become reproduced. These actions have meaning and retain meaning,
although they are routines that are part of an individual's stock of knowledge. The knowledge embedded in these routines and frames of action
become institutionalised once there is a reciprocal understanding of these
routines – something that Berger and Luckmann (*Ibid.*) call typifications.
Furthermore, these 'typifications [...] that constitute institutions are always
shared ones' (*Ibid.*, p. 55). In this way, shared understandings of ways of
doing things emerge, which become shared knowledge that shapes human
action and social order.

The way that humans understand the world therefore involves learning,
and this learning involves institutions and sets of established actions that
are created though social action. Berger and Luckmann's (1967) argument is
focused on the way that the social world is shaped by human action, yet also
appears objective and fact-like. In forming this proposition, they show that
learning about the social world, and what is perceived as nature, requires
actors to 'go out' and learn, and that this learning is then embedded within
actions, typifications and institutions. This process of knowing creates
and results in data, information and knowledge in an array of forms. What
Berger and Luckmann (*Ibid.*) demonstrate is that the world gains shape,
becomes ordered and is made understandable when data, information and
knowledge are coded in particular ways.

There is, therefore, a relationship between what we know about the
world, how we find out about the world and the ways in which we structure
that data, information and knowledge. The relationship between ontology,
epistemology and methodology is well documented in the way in which
research is practised (Hughes 1990). The outputs of particular research
practices that are built on philosophical principles result in various types
of data, which are interpreted in line with current knowledge in any one
discipline or interdisciplinary field of study (see Chapter Seven). The social
dimension of this is the way in which research is institutionalised in society
– whether in the field of science, humanities or social sciences. The question
of how to identify the particular characteristics of the institutionalisation
of research requires addressing the broader question of how research is
embedded in wider social relations and society. This logic informed the use
of disciplinary case studies within RECODE – to capture how data practices
within scientific research are embedded within wider society.

Science as an institution: Knowledge production and society

Changes in society include relationships between science and society. These changes are wider than just the relationship between science and society, because, as Merton (1973) argues, the production and role of knowledge needs to be understood through the 'modes of interplay between society, culture and science' (Merton 1973, p. 175). To illustrate the complex relationship between society, culture and science, Merton (1973) explores the relationship between the development of science and religion. Becker (1992) supports this approach and asserts that the development of science involves understanding the way that the exploration of the natural world moved from being part of 'the greater glory of God' to the role of mathematics in understanding the natural order.

In relation to this move, Merton (1973) shows that seventeenth-century English Puritanism and eighteenth-century German Pietism shaped the development of science away from a theological approach in the generation of knowledge to one where science itself has authority. This move created a shift in understanding the position of science in society, in both cultural and social terms. This can be seen in the transformation from science as a 'handmaiden' to theology during the Middle Ages to the 'modern' science of the seventeenth and eighteenth centuries. Modernity challenges established and entrenched Christian thought about science, and many of the metaphysical and theological underpinnings of science in the premodern period were questioned in modernity (Dillenberger 1960). This resulted in the change from a science that was based on Christian perspectives to a 'new science' that was founded on norms of institutional science (Merton 1968b).

The premises of modern science and the norms of institutionalised science include a detached objectivity about the research under question, a focus on logical and empirical proof (scepticism), and the following of established impersonal criteria in scientific process and towards its knowledge claims (universalism) (Becker 1992). Merton outlines some of the key characteristics of this new science or modern science, which are often called 'Cudos'. Cudos refers to four key themes of science:

- Communalism – the common ownership of scientific discoveries, according to which scientists give up intellectual property in exchange for recognition and esteem.
- Universalism – according to which claims to truth are evaluated in terms of universal or impersonal criteria, and not on the basis of race, class, gender, religion or nationality.

- Disinterestedness – according to which scientists are rewarded for acting in ways that outwardly appear to be selfless.
- Organised scepticism – all ideas must be tested and be subject to rigorous, structured community scrutiny (Merton 1942).

This shift from science as an adjunct of theology to modern science is sometimes referred to as the 'Scientific Revolution'. The transformation of science into an autonomous discipline began in Europe towards the end of the Renaissance period and continued through the late eighteenth century. This scientific turn also influenced the Enlightenment or Age of Reason – a cultural and intellectual movement based on reason, analysis and individualism.[1] There were a series of innovations in science during this period across a range of disciplines, including theories of gravitation, heliocentrism and a range of medical discoveries. The new modern science included mathematics, physics, astronomy, biology (including human anatomy) and chemistry. These disciplines featured in changing ways of understanding society and nature. The institutionalisation of modern science was marked by the establishment of the Royal Society in England in the 1660s and the Academy of Sciences in France in 1666.

One of the main features of this new science was that it sought to control and exploit nature (Cunningham and Jardine 1990). However, there was a response against modern science and the Enlightenment by the Romantic Movement in the eighteenth century, which criticised the Enlightenment's mechanistic natural philosophy. The Romantic reaction was based on a view that science should benefit both nature and society, and it advocated a 'reflective science' that would acknowledge the self in the generation of knowledge (Bossi and Poggi 1994). The focus was on how humans gain knowledge through self-understanding and working with nature (Cunningham and Jardine 1990). However, this approach declined during the 1840s with the re-establishment and further development of positivism and the strengthening of the objective scientific method. Even though there were many debates about the scientific process during the nineteenth century, such as the Popper-Kuhn debate (Fuller 2006), the practice of science became professionalised and institutionalised in ways that continue into twenty-first-century contemporary society.

---

1   The dates of the Enlightenment period are debated, but key publication dates mark its beginning and end. The beginning is marked by the publication in 1543 of Nicolaus Copernicus's *De revolutionibus orbium coelestium* (*On the Revolutions of the Heavenly Spheres*) and its end is marked by Newton's 1687 *Principia*.

Within this institutionalisation there were – and continue to be – debates about the nature of knowledge. The philosophical debates were concerned with abstract reasoning and argument, but these tended to be situated in specific historical periods, scientific and social contexts. They also included methodological debates – so the concerns were not just about what can be known (ontology), but also how we can know those things (epistemology), and in what ways we can examine these things (methodology). Toulmin (1972) traces the way that epistemology is rooted in particular historical periods and relates to the available practical procedures and to particular historically-conceived disciplines. For example, Descartes and Locke were two key figures in Western philosophy, and although they were intellectuals, they were also people of their age. They each discussed the principles of human knowledge in the context of their historical period and contemporary ideas about nature and people's place within that. This can be seen in what Toulmin (1972) calls their 'commonplaces', which is how he refers to the things these scholars took for granted. In Descartes and Locke's period, these were that:
– nature is fixed and stable;
– there is a dualism between mind and matter;
– the criterion of knowledge is a certainty built on geometry (Hughes 1990).

These 'commonplaces' provide an 'ontological description of the world and epistemological prescriptions about how the world could be investigated' (Hughes 1990, p. 8). Hughes (1990) argues that these commonplaces tend to guide and direct the work of scientists and that, over time, these commonplaces gain authority and become established views of the world. Views based on the three commonplaces cited above were widely held by scientists and philosophers at that time, and this was the basis on which further and more detailed work was undertaken in a range of disciplines. This work, in turn, gave an intellectual credibility to the underlying commonplaces. The way in which 'commonplaces' were reinforced and became justified in the scientific process was through the way that science reflexively establishes its own validity (*Ibid.*).

Part of the process of science is the interaction between developments in technology for scientific work and the way that knowledge is produced. Some technological innovations have supported the ability to discover new findings, which then create new possibilities and approaches to a range of established and emerging scientific issues. Examples of this include telescopes and calculating devices for scientific and related work. Other technological developments, such as the 'steam digester',[2] had uses beyond the laboratory and acted as precursors to – and could be patented for – wider industrial usage. These movements in science and their respective revolutions in scientific understanding resulted in changes in how the world was understood in broader society. This book argues that the role of open data in research, and the technologies and processes required to take full advantage of this data, could also bring about an evolution in technology, culture and society that informs and is informed by changes in the ways in which data are used.

Within historical worldviews of early modern science, there were many different theoretical schools as well as disciplines (for example, rationalists, empiricists and vorticists) and, even though there might be different disciplinary foci and approaches, they were nonetheless all based on a consistent ontological and epistemological framework. There was, therefore, a set of core principles that together had intellectual authority and, when strongly legitimated, form paradigms. Kuhn (1962) argues that when scientists are working within an established framework or paradigm that holds intellectual authority, they are undertaking 'normal science'. However, Kuhn (*Ibid.*) also identifies what he calls 'paradigm shift', which happens when there are anomalies that cannot be explained by the existing scientific paradigm. Kuhn (*Ibid.*) argues that paradigm is not about any one theory, but rather is a worldview in which theory exists and which frames research and knowledge production.

This discussion of the interplay between society, culture and science shows how science and the knowledge it creates is embedded within wider social and cultural processes. It also shows that there are several layers of social relations that together form the context in which the meaning of data becomes apparent. The meaning of data and he particular forms and content of data are therefore informed by the society in which that data is embedded. Part of this involves recognising the particular role of the characteristics of science in society, because its work produces distinctive senses of the natural and social world. The role of data is at the centre of shaping these senses of what is known – since data and its interpretation generates information and knowledge – and its interpretation is made possible by knowledgeable agents and social actors within particular social institutions. Given this, RECODE used precisely these agents and social actors as informants to better understand shifts in the ways in which data is

2   The steam digester was a high-pressure cooker invented by French physicist Denis Papin in 1679.

being produced, used, preserved, curated and re-used to further understand broader shifts in science, society and knowledge.

Post-industrial society: Positioning knowledge in the wider socio-economic process

The Scientific Revolution established science as a distinctive and autonomous institution and it formalised a particular process of knowledge production. Although there are debates about the scientific process and revolutions in science and in scientific paradigms, science is still seen as an autonomous institution that is responsible for developing new knowledge.[3] However, during the mid-twentieth century, changes occurred that were not so much changes in terms of the position of science as a source of knowledge, but rather shifts in where science and scientific knowledge were positioned within broader social and cultural life (Bell 1973).

During the industrial period in the Global North, the sciences and humanities knowledge base was kept within science institutions and universities. Knowledge outside of what could be referred to as the 'pure sciences' and 'disinterested scholarship' was lodged in industries such as steel making, manufacturing, mining, transportation and gas and electrical infrastructures as well as agricultural work. Although new knowledge in science and engineering contributed to developments in industry during this period, there was no direct link between science, technology and economics (MacKenzie and Wjacman 2002). However, in the mid-twentieth century, the position of science in economic life and the position of knowledge production changed. The processes of de-industrialisation and post-industrialism ushered in changes in the role of knowledge in the economy and society more broadly. Although it is highly disputed because it overemphasises change from an industrial society, Bell's (1973) work on post-industrial society points to the repositioning of knowledge in the economy, and in society more widely.

3   The rise of positivism in science was first generated during the scientific revolution and was followed by a reassertion of positivism by philosophers such as Comte in the late 1700s to mid-1800s and then further considered in the early 1900s by the Logical Positivists of the Vienna Circle as well as the Berlin Circle. The more reflective approach within science did not, however, disappear, but has followed, and continues to follow, an established anti-positivist and critical theory approach. New turns in science include more socially distributed, application-oriented, and trans-disciplinary research (Jankowski 2002).

In broad terms, a post-industrial society is one in which an economic transition has occurred from a manufacturing-based economy to a service-based economy, where there is a diffusion of national and global capital, and mass privatisation. What is distinctive about Bell's (*Ibid.*) argument is that he claims that scientific knowledge has a more central position in society. Bell (*Ibid.*) uses the notion of an axial principle to define the character of society, asserting that this acts as an energising principle for all the other dimensions of society and that, in post-industrial society, the axial principle is knowledge. In post-industrial society, Bell argues, 'theoretical knowledge' increases the importance of science and technology in the economy, which also involves the rise of professional, scientific and technical groups in society. Ritzer (1993), following on from Bell (1973), notes the growing importance of the role of scientists such as specialised engineers (genetic, electric and so on), arguing that such knowledge is seen as the basic source of innovation (for example, the knowledge created by scientists involved in the Human Genome Project is leading to new ways of treating many diseases). Advances in knowledge also produce a need for other innovations, such as ways of dealing with ethical questions raised by advances in cloning technology.

All of this involves an emphasis on theoretical rather than empirical knowledge, and on the codification of knowledge. The growth of theoretical and codified knowledge, in all its varieties, is central in the emergence of the post-industrial society. The development of new technologies also requires new intellectual technologies, which can monitor the increasingly information-driven enabled innovation, such as cybernetics, Game theory and Information theory. These processes and the new view of the role of theoretical knowledge are resulting in a new relationship between scientists and the systematic technological growth at the centre of post-industrial society. The university gains significance in such a society because it produces experts who can create, guide and control the new and dramatically-changing technologies.

Although Bell's (*Ibid.*) argument is highly debated, it does describe how the role of knowledge, scientific institutions and universities changed during the post-industrial period. The main change was that knowledge, including scientific knowledge, became more central in social and economic life. When these trends were combined with innovations such as the internet and factors including globalisation and the rise of neo-liberalism, they developed into an information society (Wessels 2014).

Information society and the knowledge economy

The move to the idea of an information society is based on the use of information and communication technologies (ICT) to manage information and communications (Webster 1995), and on the growth of the information industries (Machlup 1962). These developments prompted claims that focused specifically on information, stating that information is at the centre of the economy and thus denotes a shift away from an economy of goods into an economy of information. In this context, the organisation of information is seen as the prime creator of wealth (Porat 1977a, b). Freeman (1992, 1994) linked the development of ICT and the proliferation of information more deeply, arguing that technology is embedded within innovation cycles that produce socio-economic change. Freeman (in Mansell and Steinmuller 2000) predicted that an information-based economy was set to mature early in the twenty-first century and supports Piore and Sabel's (1984) argument that much of this economy will be characterised by flexible specialisation, in which small production units respond rapidly to niche markets with customised products made by adaptable, multi-skilled craftspeople.

This type of production is related to the idea of a network – both the network as an organisational form (Castells 2001), and as a networked society (Castells 1996). Castells (*Ibid.*) argues that the rise of networks that link people, institutions and countries characterise contemporary society. The purpose of these networks is for information to flow in what Castells (*Ibid.*) defines as an 'informationalized society' – one in which 'information generation, processing, and transmission become the fundamental sources of power and productivity' (*Ibid.*, p. 21). Castells considers this significant because it is 'the new information technology paradigm (which) provides the material basis for (the network's) pervasive expansion throughout the entire social structure' (*Ibid.*, p. 469). Thus, the network underpins and comprises the infrastructure of society. The logic of these networks is that they connect locations globally and, as Goddard (1992) argues, they provide an infrastructure for information, which is a 'key strategic resource' in the world economy. This relates to the rapid growth of the 'tradable information sector' seen in the expansion of new media and online bases of information as well as in the reorganisation of the world's financial system with the development of high finance trading. The growing 'informatization' of the economy is, with supporting policy and infrastructures, facilitating the integration of national and regional economies (Goddard, cited by Webster 1995, p. 18).

As far back as in 2000, Mansell and Steinmuller were asserting that the development of an information society would be extremely difficult to predict. They stress that any new development has to be carved out from incumbent legacies and must embrace insurgent strategies – not only for economic competitiveness and to improve political engagement, but also to facilitate a virtual community strategy that will underpin an ICT-literate society. Mansell and Steinmuller (2000) continue by arguing that these dimensions of change involve the mobilisation of society across all dimensions and require the dynamic players and emergent communities to expand the vision of an information society. This observation suggests that any analysis of an information society involves addressing broader social and economic issues, because they interact with cultural and political dynamics.

The development of an information society illustrates the way in which digital technology, social, economic and technical networks, and information are key features in contemporary society. The value of information is recognised by those in the service and finance industries as well as the information sector. Furthermore, information and its interpretation is a component in contemporary innovation. This is an important point because, in a globalised capitalised world, the economy is based on rapid innovation cycles. The information society is a speeded-up world of rapid innovation in the circulation of goods (Wessels 2010). This acceleration of innovation in an information society has generated an increasing interest in data and the ways that it could be utilised for economic purposes. This, combined with the repositioning of science and universities more centrally in the economy, created the context in which scholars could start to discuss the idea of a knowledge society.

Defining a knowledge society and changes towards Mode 2 knowledge production

Although the term 'knowledge society' was coined by Peter Drucker back in 1969, it was not developed further until the mid- to late 1990s by scholars such as Robin Mansell (1998) and Nico Stehr (1994). Instead, as discussed above, change was discussed in terms of an information society and in many ways that focus is apt because the term 'knowledge society' is distinctive and differs from the definitions of an information society. Discussions about the information society tend to focus on commercial and economic networks in society. There has, of course, been some commentary about the social and cultural aspects of such a society, which indicate that digital processes and digital content are pervasive and integrated into daily life (Wessels 2010). Nonetheless, the strong focus on economic networks and information in discussions about an information society misses some of the claims made by the developer of the World Wide Web (WWW), who suggested that the WWW could open up society and enable the sharing of information and data freely amongst people (Berners Lee 1999).

Mansell (1998) and Stehr (1994) note that the debates about an information society cannot be separated from considerations about a knowledge society. This is because the notions of information society rest, to some degree, on commercial and economic networks of society that are technologically supported, whereas the concept of knowledge society encompasses other dimensions, such as ethical and political concerns within social life. Yet, despite these social issues being raised, most attention has been paid to notions of an information society and a knowledge economy – and further, little attention has been paid to how they relate to each other. The most well-established approach is Castells' (2001), stating that the organisational form underpinning both a knowledge economy and an information society is the network based on digital technology. Castells (2001) clearly states the potential that an informational and networked society would have if there was an appropriate institutional framework that would support an inclusive society. However, he notes that there are also negative aspects of informational and networked developments, which include concerns such as greater control and administrative power through surveillance of populations, greater inequality in terms of both production and consumption, and challenges for ensuring privacy. The points Castells raises are made in relation to an information society scenario. These points are still relevant when discussing the knowledge society today.

Currently, there is no agreed definition of 'knowledge society', so the term is often used to refer to a range of possible concepts of a knowledge society. The term or similar terms, are not new. Back in 1966, Robert Lane used the phrase 'knowledgeable society' to refer to the growing social relevance of scientific knowledge. His view relates tightly to a specific understanding of science during the early 1960s, which thought that science would enhance social life by replacing common sense with scientific reasoning. He draws parallels with the political sphere, arguing that democratic society is founded on governmental and interpersonal relations as well as the affluent society, which is built on an economic foundation. His concept is based on the normative framework for science as set out by Robert Merton and he considered that a knowledgeable society would be rooted in epistemology and the logic of inquiry. Drucker (1969) defines the term 'knowledge society' in a more open way, placing the role of knowledge at the centre of society, where it provides the basis for the economy and social action. These early concepts about a knowledge society dovetail closely with Daniel Bell's (1973) thesis, that knowledge is at the centre of society, and they lay a foundation for the notion that, in late modernity, 'knowledge' in seen in terms of both codified knowledge and scientific knowledge.

These early definitions and conceptions of knowledge society are based on a Mertonian understanding of science. Furthermore, they reflect the optimism and belief that science had the power to transform society that was prevalent in the mid-1900s. However, not only has the world stage changed in social, economic and political senses, but science and the practice of science has also changed. Gibbons, Limoges, Nowotny, Schwartzman, Scott and Trow published '*The New Production of Knowledge: The dynamics of science and research in contemporary societies*' in 1994, which examined changes in forms of knowledge production. The authors proposed that there had been a move in knowledge production from what they termed 'Mode 1' to 'Mode 2' knowledge production. Although their thesis simplified the changes and practices, it did nonetheless sensitise commentators and policymakers to an apparent trend. Mode 1 was characterised by 'the hegemony of theoretical or, at any rate, experimental science; by an internally-driven taxonomy of disciplines; and by the autonomy of scientists and their host institutions, the universities' (Nowotny, Scott and Gibbons 2003, p. 179). Mode 2 was seen as a new paradigm of knowledge production that is characterised by 'socially distributed, application-oriented, trans-disciplinary, and subject to multiple accountabilities' (*Ibid.*).

The 'Mode 1 to Mode 2' thesis was well received by policymakers, who were looking for better ways to link science with innovation, with professional disciplines such as management studies, and with researchers in new universities or institutions outside of the traditional university and scientific system. The argument was not so well received, however, by researchers based in what we can term 'the establishment of science' – that is, those working in established scientific disciplines and institutions – who sought to retain their autonomy. These groups were concerned that the quality of the science might be compromised through the more open levelling of ideas, and they feared that their own autonomy would be under threat if there were closer links between research and innovation (Nowotny, Scott and Gibbons, 2003). The main controversy around this book was that the move from Mode 1 to Mode 2 proposed a move to relativism, which undermined the established scientific adherence to objectivity within specific paradigms. To respond to these concerns, Nowotny, Scott and Gibbons further developed their thinking and wrote '*Rethinking Science: Knowledge and the Public in an Age of Uncertainty*' in 2001. In this book, the authors sought to defend

some of the characteristics of academic discourse, whilst analysing how that discourse was being changed. To do this, they identify three trends that are part of a changing research environment:
- The tighter steering of research priorities at supranational and national level.
- The commercialisation of research or 'engaged' research.
- The accountability of research.

The effects of these trends are feeding into a new discourse of science and into the role of scientific institutions within discourse (see Chapter Five regarding their role in open data). The drive for a more engaged science whose impact can be measured has resulted in the demise of what is variously termed as 'pure', 'blue skies' or 'disinterested' research. This is illustrated in the UK through the government's research assessment exercises, which include lay appraisers as well as expert reviewers, and the call for detailed impact studies and evaluations (Nowotny, Scott and Gibbons, 2003). Nowotny, Scott and Gibbons (*Ibid.*) argue that this change means that knowledge is no longer seen as a public good, but rather is seen as intellectual property, 'which is produced, accumulates, and traded like other goods and services in the knowledge society' (Ibid. 2003, p. 185). In this process, they argue, a new language has been created – one of application, relevance, contextualisation, outreach, technology transfer and knowledge management. These changes have been met with various responses, from a 'literature of regret' as articulated by the Campaign for Academic Freedom and Democracy (now http://www.cafas.org.uk/) and other concerns of academic scientists.

Another response that is contrary to the one above is the literature of 'modernisation', which stresses the importance of research in a knowledge society (Nowotny, Scott and Gibbons, 2003). This literature stresses the need to align research priorities with social, economic and political priorities which, in the UK, was articulated in the White Paper: *'Realising Our Potential'*. Although this paper proposed a high-level focus on change in knowledge production, there was no attempt to make a deeper analysis of the changes in knowledge production in terms of how knowledge is produced, validated and disseminated (*Ibid.*). This meant that the inner core of the practice and framework of research was not addressed and was seen to be in the domain of the scientific community. This combination of changes to the role and position of science, the way that knowledge is produced, assessed and shared, how research is practiced, alongside developments in an economy based on knowledge, are all constitutive of society. Despite all these changes, though, one question remains: how do these changes relate to Drucker's point that knowledge also underpins the ability for agency and social action?

Stehr (1994) picks up on the fact that this idea of knowledge underpinning agency and social action is not fully considered in debates about information society or transformations to a knowledge society. He notes that the focus tends to be on an information society and knowledge economy agenda, rather than fully considering what would constitute a knowledge society. He starts by asking what the distinction might be between a knowledge society and what he terms a 'science society' (which includes many of the characteristics of information society and post-industrial society). His choice of term is important since he builds on the discussion cited above, noting that the main concerns of these are the 'production, processing, and transmission of a very large amount of data about all sorts of matter – individual and national, social and commercial, economic and military' (Stehr 1994, p. 12). Taking into account that information in various forms has always been part of society historically, and continues to be so, Stehr (1994) points to some of the gaps in the analysis of knowledge society. He notes that there is little discussion about the genesis of the information's substance or about changes brought about by the information's content. Furthermore, there is a lack of attention to questions the use of data in regard to solidarity or domination in society – data can be used to foster an open participative solidarity and society, or can also be used dominate and oppress people in society in repressive regimes (*Ibid.*). Stehr (*Ibid.*) analyses changes in terms of the forms and dominance of knowledge, addressing knowledge and science and then going beyond that, to assess the relationship between scientific and everyday knowledge, and knowledge as a capacity for social action.

To do this, Stehr (1994) suggests that there is a need to address the specifics of knowledge to identify how that knowledge can be used in society, by whom and for whom. This extends beyond the rather narrow focus of post-industrial or information society analyses, which consider the position of knowledge on the one hand and the way it can be distributed on the other hand. Stehr (1994) puts aside the point that discussions about how the impact of science serves the development of an assessment of the value of science (Holzner *et al.* 1987), to consider its impact more widely. He writes that, in 'most conventional accounts, science is said to generate, first and foremost, if not exclusively, new types of possibilities for, or constraints on, practical action' (Stehr 1994, p. 12). He expands on this by considering:

- That science and technology not only allow for new forms of action but they also eliminate others and have an impact on the experience of action.
- They also assure the 'survival' (in the sense of continued relevance) of existing forms of action and, in some sense, even generate occasions that affirm traditional action (Stehr 1994, p. 13).

This focus goes beyond scientific and technological determinism, whilst recognising that science and technology do feature in change and continuity. What Stehr (1994) seeks to show is that, in knowledge societies, science and technology can be used as agents of change, but can also be used to resist homogeneous transformation. What this suggests is that science and technology have 'enabling features' that 'increase the number of available strategies, heighten flexibility or effect the ability of the powerful to exercise control and constraining forces which limit choices, reduce options and impose penalties and risks' (*Ibid.*, p. 13). Scientific knowledge as well as other types of knowledge, can therefore both enable and constrain social action and, when knowledge of various forms becomes a central feature in societies – such as a proposed knowledge society – then those societies become both 'more standardised and more fragile' (*Ibid.*). Therefore, defining what a knowledge society is requires going beyond the definitions of information society – whilst recognising their legacy – by recognising the way in which 'knowledge' features in social action, how it can be generated, shared and acted upon by social groups. This means addressing the concrete ways in which knowledge is produced and consumed, by examining the politics of data and data sharing, because who has access to data and can interpret it influences how data can be used in generating knowledge. It also determines who has knowledge and who has the capacity and capability – the agency – to use it.

In overall terms, Stehr (1994, 2004, 2012) argues that the development of a knowledge society is a gradual process that is not deliberately triggered by human design, but, instead, is shaped by the ways that new technologies, new data fields, new needs and new imaginations interact and configure to produce new possibilities and innovations. In the consideration of the knowledge society, there is a need to define what knowledge means in the context of such as society. Stehr defines knowledge as a capacity for action which, he argues, has multifaceted implications. For example, some knowledge may not be used and knowledge can be employed for irrational ends as well as for progressive purposes. Stehr's (1994) definition of knowledge as a capacity for action indicates that the material realisation and implementation of knowledge is open and is dependent on, or embedded within, the context of specific social, economic and intellectual traditions. In general terms, knowledge is different from information in that it requires frameworks or commonplaces and resources to create it as well as the intellectual and cultural interpretation to analyse it and put the data to use.

A broad definition of knowledge is also evident in the way the term has been used in some policy documents, especially those published by UNESCO. The 'UNESCO World Report' (2005) claims that 'knowledge' needs to be considered as an object that has huge stakes in society in economic, political and cultural terms. The report raises some critical points about the kind of knowledge implied in a knowledge society, and it questions a techno-scientific definition of knowledge. Instead, the report asserts that there are different types of knowledge, such as local knowledge, for example. It also highlights the inequalities of access to knowledge and capacities to interpret and use it. In this context, UNESCO makes some ethical and normative suggestions within a development paradigm, claiming that, to 'remain human and liveable, knowledge societies will have to be societies of shared knowledge' (*Ibid*.). It is thus arguing for an open approach to knowledge, with data being a central part of this dynamic. Relating to the ideal of a knowledge society being a progressive open society there are, of course, a range of understandings about knowledge society that are more restrictive while, in the struggle between standardisation and fragility, there is a strong call from regional to global policy actors for 'activating knowledge' (Soete 1997). This call raises questions about how knowledge can be activated and by whom.

Conclusion

The Scientific Revolution challenged the role that existing institutions such as the church played as the key source of knowledge and authority, instead designating science and the institution of science as the primary place for the growth of knowledge. The way in which knowledge was, and is, produced creates debate within broader social and cultural life and during social and cultural change. For example, Kuhn focused on science as a knowledge enterprise, whilst Popper gave science symbolic importance because it expressed a critical rationality that was relevant to all aspects of life. The role of science is also positioned politically in terms of its funding and contribution to society, as seen in Mode 2 knowledge production. As the role of scientific knowledge grew in society, and continues to grow, it has become incorporated into many aspects of society (Stehr 1994). However, the level at which knowledge is integrated into society is limited and this is especially the case in terms of access to data, including scientific data. So, although the position of science in society has changed, access to scientific data is controlled by the scientific community. Therefore, not only do the social relations of a society – its institutions and their agency – shape the way that knowledge is produced, they also interpret the role of science in society. This role goes beyond the focus on knowledge production towards considering the economic, social and environmental roles of science, which are discussed in more detail in Chapters Six and Nine. This relates to Berger and Luckmann's (1967) thesis on the way shared understandings of ways of doing things are created and, thus, the way that shared knowledge shape human action and social order.

The RECODE project examined each of these theoretical issues through the lens of recent approaches to providing open access to the data generated by scientific research practice. It examined how this changing understanding of data is being shaped by larger policy changes within particular political contexts (e.g. Europe, the USA and Australia) and how this reflects and reinforces new relationships between science, society and culture. This is evidenced by the changing nature of knowledge production that positions data as a product or piece of intellectual property rather than a means to a scientific conclusion and an imperative to treat data as a commodity and manage it accordingly. RECODE also examines how technology functions as both a push and a pull factor to enable and promote changes in producing, managing and re-using scientific data. Finally, it examines authoritative figures within these practices, including scientists, librarians, policymakers and industry and how their perspectives are integrated, including how this compares to those of actors with less relative influence within these spaces, e.g. students, activists, citizens and others.

3.   Visions of open data

Introduction

In this chapter, we argue that the value of data is realised through its own characteristics and by the way it can be used in particular contexts. To address how data and open data may have value requires understanding data, data types and how data is constituted and open for use. Policymakers, scientists, government and civil society organisations are all developing definitions and understandings of data and open data. There is some variation, but each of these actors is contributing to the general understanding. Once the characteristics of data are understood, then it is important to examine how data may be used to develop a knowledge society. This means considering what the social relations of mobilisation are, by addressing data ecosystems in research processes. In this chapter, we consider three types of data: open research data, open government data and big data.

The chapter traces the ways that data and open data have been defined by different actors from civil society, from government and in the context of big data. It considers the diverse aspirations that these actors have about how open data may contribute to social, economic and political life. In line with each of these, ideas about data ecosystems are outlined – again – from within each community's perspective and approach to change. What is distinctive is that the way data is being considered links to actors within key communities, who are also linked to mobilising open data. Thus, the way that open data is being considered relates to a range of actors who are seeking to mobilise open data. There is, therefore, a close link between discussions about data and about social movements in terms of an open data movement, as the next chapter explores. Both of these dimensions – open data and social movements pushing for open data – relate to visions of a knowledge society, as discussed in Chapter Two.

Civil society and open data

Definitions of open data build on the very broad definitions of data[1] and, in an overall sense, open data describes data that is openly available – i.e. accessible,

---

1   Data as a concept can be viewed as the lowest level of abstraction from which information and, then, knowledge are derived. In general terms, data is a set of values of qualitative or

understandable and open to reuse (Wessels *et al.* 2014). These aspects of open data are drawn together by civil society organisation Open Knowledge Foundation (OKF), its network Open Knowledge Foundation Network (OKFN) (renamed Open Knowledge International in 2016) in order to link data with the production of knowledge. The OKFN is an organisation that is seeking to enable open access to data and, particularly, to relate open data to open knowledge. Its definition of open knowledge links closely to Stehr's (1994) argument about a knowledge society, stating that 'open knowledge' is 'any content, information or data that people are free to use, re-use and redistribute – without any legal, technological or social restriction' (https://okfn.org/opendata/). OKFN argues that open data are the building blocks of open knowledge: 'Open knowledge is what open data becomes when it's useful, usable and used' (*Ibid.*).

The OKFN has also developed a clear outline of the key characteristics of open knowledge:

– Availability and access: the data must be available as a whole, preferably by downloading over the internet, and at no more than a reasonable reproduction cost. The data must also be available in a convenient and modifiable form.
– Reuse and redistribution: the data must be provided under terms that permit reuse and redistribution, including intermixing with other datasets. The data must be machine-readable.
– Universal participation: everyone must be able to use, reuse and redistribute – there should be no discrimination against fields of endeavour or against persons or groups.
   For example, 'non-commercial' restrictions that would prevent 'commercial' use, or restrictions of use for certain purposes (e.g. only in education), are not allowed (*Ibid.*).

The OKFN also looks across a wide range of data, thus pushing the issue of open data beyond science data, and identifies the following kinds of data that can play a role in open knowledge:

– Cultural: data about cultural works and artefacts – for example titles and authors – which is generally collected and held by galleries, libraries, archives and museums.
– Science: data that is produced as part of scientific research – from any discipline.

---

quantitative variables. The presence of data, as something already found or something created through research processes or as a by-product of social action, is seen to have value either in itself or in its reuse.

–   Finance: data such as government accounts (expenditure and revenue) and information on financial markets (stocks, shares, bonds, etc.).
–   Statistics: data produced by statistical offices, such as the census and key socio-economic indicators.
–   Weather: the many types of information used to understand and predict the weather and climate.
–   Environment: information related to the natural environment, such as the presence and level of pollutants, or the quality of and rivers and seas.
–   Transport: data such as timetables, routes, on-time statistics (*Ibid.*).

The OKFN outlines some of the reasons why it considers open data and open knowledge important. It argues that open data has the potential to support transparency, to realise social and commercial value and enhance participation and engagement. In terms of transparency, the organisation argues that citizens need to know what governments doing to ensure a functioning, democratic society. For people to be able to find this out, the OKFN argues, citizens must have free access to government data and information and be able to share that information with other citizens. This argument therefore assumes that transparency is not just about access, but is also about sharing and reuse. This means that there is a need for analytical tools, including visualisation tools, to be open to all, so that the data can be freely used and reused. In terms of releasing social and commercial value, the OKFN places the role of data firmly in a digital age of data collection and curation.

The OKFN draws on a digital society position, which argues that data is a key resource for social and commercial activities. Data – whether digitised or created in digital form – is pervasive, as are digital systems for storing and circulating data, and their contexts of use can range from providing directions to a local post office or building an international search engine. Both these examples require access to data, much of which is created or held by governments. Given the OKFN's position on open knowledge, it is supporting the UK's open government agenda. The organisation asserts that, by making data available to everyone, the government can help drive the creation of innovative business and services that deliver social and commercial value. Access to data that can be shared and reused is also seen as supporting participation and engagement in social and political life. In this sphere, the OKFN suggests that open data can be used to support participatory governance and to improve the way that businesses and organisations engage with users and audiences. A central area of participation that the organisation points to is citizen engagement. In this context, the OKFN argues that citizens usually only engage sporadically with politics, for instance, by voting in national elections every four or five years. However, the OKFN asserts that, 'by opening up data, citizens are enabled to be much more directly informed and involved in decision-making' (*Ibid.*). This is an example of how mobilising data is seen as having the potential to transform social relations. As the OKFN argues, open data can go beyond making government transparent, because it enables citizens to know what is happening within government, but also enables them to make informed contributions to government processes and decision making (*Ibid.*). The OKFN suggests that this moves society on, by making it a full 'read/write' society.

This last point illustrates the way in which some organisations such as the OKFN and other civil society organisations, such as the Open Rights Foundation, Open Forum Foundation and the Sunlight Foundation, are key social actors in mobilising open data. These types of organisations go beyond merely making data open, through their vision of open knowledge that can contribute to an open and knowledgeable society. This can be seen in the way that the OKFN has generated a more holistic 'open defini-tion', which clarifies the OKFN's vision: 'the precise meaning of 'open' that clearly focuses on knowledge and open in this context involves generating and promoting a 'robust commons in which anyone may participate, and interoperability is maximised' (OKFN 2015). The vision and principle driving this organisation is that knowledge is only open if 'anyone is free to access, use, modify, and share it – subject, at most, to measures that preserve provenance and openness' (*Ibid.*). The organisation argues that this links with other related definitions of open, such as open source software which is embedded within internet and World Wide Web culture (Berners Lee 1991; Castells 2001), and which is synonymous with 'free' or 'libre', as defined by Free Cultural Works.[2]

There is, therefore, a strong push – and an ideological vision – that moti-vates the OKFN as an organisation. To some degree, it is part of a movement – along with others in its civil society network – seeking to drive open data and open knowledge. However, in order to achieve this goal, there need to

2   Free Cultural Works are works or expressions which can be freely studied, applied, copied and/or modified, by anyone, for any purpose. This term also describes certain permissible restrictions that respect or protect these essential freedoms. The definition distinguishes between free works, and free licences, which can be used to legally protect the status of a free work. The definition itself is not a licence; it is a tool to determine whether a work or licence should be considered 'free': http://creativecommons.org/freeworks.

be protocols in place to ensure that data is made open in a responsible way. There are some well-established criteria that organisations, repositories and individuals are increasingly aware of, such as licensing – that is, the legal conditions under which data is made available (see Chapter Eight). When there is no provision for a licence then the working position taken is that potential users of the data need to abide by existing legal conditions governing use of the work, for example, copyright or public domain requirements (https://okfn.org/opendata/).

However, for data to be open – what the OKFN calls 'open works' – a set of specific conditions must be satisfied, including the requirement that the work must have an open licence. Furthermore, the entire work should be accessible at a fair reproduction cost, or be freely available on the WWW, alongside all the necessary information regarding complying with the work's licence. The aim of these licences is to allow free reuse and redistribution of all, or parts of the work. It must also allow for derivatives of the work to be made, to be subsequently distributed or compiled with any other works. The licence must allow use, redistribution, modification and compilation for any purpose. The rights attached to the work must apply to anyone it is redistributed to, without the need to agree to any additional legal terms. There may be some clauses that ask for attribution to be cited for those who produced the work. There is often a share-alike clause that requires copies or derivatives of a licenced work to remain under a licence that is the same as, or similar to the original. In general terms, this approach requires any licence to avoid discriminating against any person or group and must ensure that the works are free, so that there are no royalty charges or fee arrangements of any sort (*Ibid.*).

There is also a focus on open format, which means that the data needs to be stored in a convenient and modifiable form to ensure that there are no technological obstacles to people making use of the licenced rights. This means that the data needs to be machine-readable, available in bulk, stored in an open format (i.e. a format with a freely-available published specification that places no restrictions – monetary or otherwise – on its use) or, at the very least, can be processed with at least one free/libre/open-source software tool. There are some checks to ensure that licenced works adhere to this, which may prohibit distribution of the work in a manner where technical measures would impose restrictions on the exercise of otherwise allowed rights (*Ibid.*). These licence details show that a range of legal, technical and data standards must be followed, in order to facilitate open data and, consequently, open knowledge.

In sum, advocates of open data and civil society organisations have been influential in promoting the idea of open data, and they have linked this to visions of open knowledge. They have created a range of ideals to illustrate some of the potential that open knowledge has for society, and have developed protocols to support their realisation. Many of these protocols are closely linked to the 'grand challenges' examined by RECODE, including technology barriers, cultural barriers, legal and ethical issues and institutional and policy issues. By recognising and addressing these, the OKFN's ambitions align well with some visions of a knowledge society, in that they seek to make data openly available for everyone in society. However, even if some of the problematic issues around making data open have been addressed, it still requires access to a range of data, including government data and research data, for a transformation to open knowledge to be achieved. The vision of open data and open knowledge propounded by civil society organisations will not be fully realised without open government data and open research data, which will be discussed next.

Open government data

Open government data is a relatively new concept, and the term 'Open Government Data (OGD)' only became widely-used after 2008 (Ubaldi 2013). It emerged in the United States, from the work of a group of open data advocates including Tim O'Reilly, Lawrence Lessig and Aaron Swartz. There were 30 members of the Open Government Group (OGG) (http://resource. org/8_principles.html) who met in October 2007 to develop some open data principles and to discuss how they could mobilise people who were interested in developing citizen training in data management, curation and use.

The group developed eight principles that underpin the two main elements of open government data, which are that:
–   Government data is any data and information produced or commissioned by public bodies.
–   Open data are data that can be freely used, reused and distributed by anyone, only subject to (at the most) the requirement that users attribute the data to their producers and that they also make their work available to be shared (Ubaldi 2013).

The remit of data in government work has been shaped through the concept of Public Sector Information (PSI), which is defined as 'information including information products and services, generated, created, collected, processed, preserved, maintained, disseminated, or funded by or for a government or public institution' (OECD 2008). Although the definition of data is fairly broad, OGD focuses on some specific data sets. These include business information; registers, patent and trademark information and public tender databases; geographic information; legal information; meteorological information; social data, and transport information.

The eight OGD principles are similar in intent to the guidelines laid down by the OKFN. The OGG notes the importance of adhering to a set of principles to ensure that making data open is done in a responsible way. The group argue that government data can only be considered open if it is made public by complying with the following principles:

1. Complete: all public data are made available. Public data are data that is not subject to valid privacy, security or privilege limitations.
2. Primary: data are as collected at source, with the highest possible level of granularity, not in aggregate or modified forms.
3. Timely: data are made available as quickly as necessary to preserve the value of the data.
4. Accessible: data are available to the widest range of users for the widest range of purposes.
5. Machine processable: data are reasonably structured to allow automated processing.
6. Non-discriminatory: data are available to everyone, with no requirement for registration
7. Non-proprietary: data are available in a format over which no entity has exclusive control.
8. Licence-free: data are not subject to any copyright, patent, trademark or trade secret regulation. Reasonable privacy, security and privilege restrictions may be allowed (http://resource.org/8_principles.html).

These principles, often called the 'Sebastopol List' after the place in California where they were developed, were developed further in 2011 by the US Federal Chief Information Officer Vivek Kundra and by the UK's Public Sector Transparency Board in 2012. These have extended the eight principles, but are based on the recommendations made in the original Sebastopol List.

OGD is a rapidly-growing area. Tim Davies (2013), for example, notes that, in the early 2000s, few governments had engaged with the idea of open data, and the number of OGD initiatives could be counted on one hand. However, by mid-2013, he reports that the concept of OGD had spread across the globe (*Ibid.*). Davies' 'OGD Report' (2013) shows that OGD portals and projects can now be found on every continent, and in an increasing number of cities and

in international institutions. Open data is now part of many strategies and actions plans at the highest levels, including:
–   Open Government partnership national action plans.
–   G8 Open Data Charter.
–   Open data in aid, extractives and agriculture.
–   'UN High Level Report on the Post-2015 Development Agenda', which calls for a 'data revolution', incorporating a move towards open data.

Despite this dramatic progress, however, Davies comments that diffusion of the open data idea has not been experienced equally across geographies and sectors; nor have the potential benefits of open data been locked-in. There is still a long way to go before the democratic, social and economic potentials of open data can be fully realised in every country, and – even where contextual factors are conducive to open data supply and use – many OGD initiatives are presently resting on shallow foundations, at risk of stalling or falling backwards if political will or community pressure subsides (Davies 2013).

Similar to the OKFN's position, there is a social, civic and economic rationale to the development of OGD, since it focuses on creating value that takes the argument beyond making data accessible. Although the Organisation for Economic Cooperation and Development (OECD) made a strong argument in 2012 that the amount of data available in the current information economy is exploding, national governments are also focusing on increasing the transparency of their processes and performance. Governments seek to achieve this by making their official data available in machine-readable linked data sets that can be searched and reused using standard tools. This process of open – both data and the means to search and manipulate it – is seen as a critical new resource for making changes in value creation, in economic, social and political terms (Ubalbi 2013). Ubalbi (*Ibid.*) asserts that the economic and social case for OGD is well established and is now backed up by evidence from UK and US national and local governments in particular. There is some belief that OGD will also create value in political and social terms, although this is, as yet, more difficult to evidence.

When considering value, it is important to ask who might benefit from new forms of value creation; it is, therefore, a question of 'value for whom'? In general terms, PSI is understood to be a strategic resource that has potential for a number of stakeholders, such as: public sector organisations, private sector businesses, academia, citizens and civic organisations (*Ibid.*). Benefits of open data for government are often seen at the macro level and are largely couched in terms of changing the way that governments can undertake their roles and responsibilities. Open data is thought to be useful in decision making and in allocating resources to support more efficient government. There are also drives to use open data to make government services more effective, efficient, smarter and personalised. However, open data has the ability to contribute to more than just efficiency and service delivery objectives – it can also improve government transparency, which will help citizens hold their governments to account. Furthermore, open data – or when implemented within government processes as open government – can help governments to achieve and retain legitimacy with individual citizens and civil society. From the citizens' point of view, OGD is seen as having the potential to enable the co-development and co-production of services, and to allow citizens to acquire information and knowledge from a wider range of sources. Supporters of OGD believe that these types of activities bring additional benefits for citizens, such as supporting their greater participation and engagement in civic life (*Ibid.*).

OGD provides the foundation for a range of activities and initiatives within civil society, with the value being felt more keenly in OECD countries. In this context, there is a focus on realising the benefits of OGD for the public as well as the government. There are many civil society organisations that each concentrate on a particular area of OGD. These include the Sunlight Foundation (US) and the Open Knowledge Foundation (Germany), the Open Rights Foundation (UK) and the Open Forum Foundation (US). These groups' foci include increasing transparency and improving services, which aligns well with the open government agenda. Other areas are supporting vulnerable groups, protecting the environment and supporting sustainable growth. These organisations often make a contribution by identifying how open data could produce high value.

Although OGD is a global issue, its development globally is uneven. As Davies (2013) reports, the development of an open government data community of stakeholders and users is fragmented and uneven across the world. This is partly the result of different levels of resources, funding and readiness, but it also relates to different perceptions of what OGD is and what it should do. For example, entrepreneurs are seeking frameworks and processes that support reuse and reliable licensing, whilst programmers want raw data. Others, such as data activists, are looking for access to government documents, whereas citizens may want secondary information products and civil society organisations are keen to have access to data sets that they can combine, to improve service delivery and the quality of life of particular social groups (Ubalbi 2013).

As a result, the impact that open data can have is still unclear, as noted in the '2013 Open Data Barometer Global Report' (Davies 2013). This report identifies some key barriers that hinder access to open data and reduce its potential impact. In particular, the report raises the broader issues of infrastructure, legal and regulatory frameworks, data management and depositing as well as the lack of integration in developments. The report suggests that some specific gaps need to be addressed, including:

– The uneven and fragmented development of open access. The report found that current developments take many forms, ranging from isolated open data portals within an e-government framework to ambitious, government-wide open government data implementation.
– There is a lack of data being published in machine-readable form and under open licence.
– None of the 77 countries surveyed for the Open Data Barometer can claim to be 'open by default' (see the report for the list of countries covered).
– There is a lack of key data sets and ability to reuse the data from the Barometer's middle-ranked countries.
– Some countries lack robust right to information laws, which undermines people's confidence in open access to research data.
– Low-ranking countries and developing countries do not have well-managed and digitised government data sets (*Ibid.*, p. 3).

In sum, OGD focuses on the ways that open access to data can improve relationships between citizens and their governments. It is less radical and transformative than the visions of some open knowledge organisations in civil society. Nonetheless, advocates of OGD aspire towards attaining more open and transparent government, and facilitating citizens to use public data to improve their knowledge and engage with public issues in a more informed way. However, progress in OGD has been uneven across the globe, in ways that may reproduce – or even increase – existing inequalities. This risk runs counter to some of the progressive visions of a knowledge society, which believe that knowledge can be most effective when used by those who have the most resources to harness the value of data.

Open research data

The term 'research data' is defined in just as broad terms as 'data', but, in general, research data is any material used as a foundation for research.

The OECD defines research data as any kind of resource that is useful to researchers (OECD 2007), while the European Commission (EC) states that research data 'may be numerical/quantitative, descriptive/ qualitative or visual, raw or analysed, experimental or observational, examples include digitized primary research data, photographs and images, films, etc.' (European Commission 2012). Thus, data can be in the form of published texts, artefacts or raw unprocessed data.

These broad definitions of data underpin both definitions of open research data and open access to research data (Wessels *et al.* 2014). The open research data policy community draws on the Berlin Declaration, which states that open access contributions include original scientific research results, raw data and metadata, source materials, digital representations of pictorial and graphical materials and scholarly multimedia material (Max Planck Society 2003). The EC's definition of 'Open Access' is 'free [...] access to and use of publicly-funded scientific publications and data' (EC 2012). The views of these policymakers extend beyond making certain types of research data open by explaining how data is made open. This point is illustrated in the remit of the Declaration for Open Access, which states that authors and rights holders must grant users free access to the materials, including a licence to copy, use, distribute and display that material, subject to proper attribution of authorship and responsible use. Furthermore, data needs to be curated as a complete version of the work, in an appropriate standard format and submitted to an online repository with suitable technical standards that enable open access, unrestricted distribution, interoperability, and long-term archiving (Wessels *et al.* 2014).

Thus, making research data open means extending access to that data beyond its producers and the producer community. It includes considering issues such as how the data can be accessed, in what formats and from which types of repositories. The value of the data, therefore, depends not only on its characteristics and quality, but also on how it is managed and curated, so how accessible it is. From a broad policy perspective, the purpose of open data is to extend access to data and to support wider use of data. The Berlin Declaration envisages open access to research data that has the potential to create 'a comprehensive source of human knowledge and cultural heritage that has been approved by the scientific community' (Max Planck Society 2003). Bringing together the range of data, its management and curating, the Royal Society (2012) defines open data as data that is accessible, usable, assessable and able to be evaluated. The Royal Society's (2012) definition shows that data can provide value not only through the process of its creation and what that may tell researchers who are part of that process, but also in the ways that the data can be assessed and evaluated. This point relates to the previous chapter's discussion about the rigour of scientific process in generating knowledge.

These broad definitions of data – especially research data – when combined with definitions of open data or open access to data, show the way in which data is being considered by policymakers. The general move towards perceiving research as part of Mode 2 knowledge production within an information society context means that data is viewed in a different way to that found in Mode 1. This argument asserts that if data is produced through publically-funded research, then stakeholders, communities, businesses and individual citizens have a right to access it. Furthermore, according to Mode 2 knowledge production, data is seen as having value through its reuse by a wider range of users than just the research community that produced the data.

The perceived benefits of open access include giving researchers the ability to subsequently make use of the data for further research, as data reuse prevents costly duplication of data gathering efforts. Open access may permit more data to be brought into complex, interdisciplinary areas of enquiry and enable the validation of research results, for example by assisting reproducibility and ensuring quality control. Policymakers could use the data to inform decision making, while the private sector could use it to develop new products and services. Civil society organisations (CSOs) and citizens would have access to data in order to become better informed about important scientific developments and to participate in public debates. Although such benefits are laudable, open access raises some concerns about the functioning of research ecosystems that underpin the rigour of research (Sveindottir *et al.* 2013).

Another aspect of the development of open access to data is the growth of 'e-research' (Jankowski 2009), which refers to the use of digital technologies to support new and existing forms of research and research practice. This is fostering a reconsideration of the way that scientific and scholarly knowledge is produced and shared. The practice of research rests on a model of open inquiry, which was traditionally worked through via publication of peer-reviewed research results, where primary data was not always openly shared. However, the development of digital means of producing, storing and manipulating data is creating a focus on 'data-led science' (Royal Society 2012), which requires data to be shared and made openly available.

In broad terms, open access to research data refers to making various types of data openly available to public and private stakeholders, user communities and citizens. This initiative, however, involves more than simply providing easier and wider access to data for potential user groups. The development of open access involves a reconsideration of the entire system of knowledge production and dissemination, which can be seen in the way in which research ecosystems are developing to support open research data. Open access to research data is improving within academia; however, access to data for those outside academia is still in its infancy, and this area is discussed in more detail in Chapter Six. The picture inside academia itself is mixed. There are some areas – particularly in the environmental sciences (as discussed in Chapter Seven) – that welcome the principals of open data, and some share the vision of an open knowledge society. However, in contrast, many academics still believe that data is best shared with peers who have the skills to interpret the data.

Commercial sector and big data[3]

The development of big data is a relatively new phenomenon and, although the term is debated, the first definition clearly identifies its distinctive features: big data requires high management capabilities and is characterised by the '3Vs' – Volume, Velocity and Variety (Laney 2001). Big data is derived from a range of digital technologies, communication, media and services. Thus, open data, the public web, social media, mobile applications, geospatial data, and commercial databases are all sources of data which aggregate individual data from both commercial and openly-accessible sources, data from sensors (in space, and in-situ), web-enabled devices (the Internet of Things) as well as a whole range of digitally-based services that constitute the many sources of big data.

The big data phenomenon is still in a relatively early phase of development, so its potential value is not yet fully understood and, as discussed in Chapter Nine, is being more critically addressed after the early hype about it. However, estimates include that of Turner *et al.* (2014), who suggest that the 'digital universe' will grow at 40 per cent a year for the next decade, reaching 44 trillion gigabytes over the next decade. They argue that this growth will be driven, in particular, by the billions of new internet-enabled sensors and embedded devices, most of which are on mobile units. Furthermore, these devices have automatically-generated tags (metadata), which mean that their data content will add to the data available and, therefore, increase even more rapidly the amount of information available and data that may

3   Many thanks to Max Craglia for his insights and contributions to this section.

have the potential to be useful for analysis. These early indicators of growth feed into claims about the impacts and overall benefits of big data (e.g. Vesset *et al.* 2012; EMA/9sights 2013). For example, the EMA/9sights' 2013 report argues that initiatives to integrate big data into the fabric of everyday business operations are growing in importance. These include integrating advanced analytics, such as customer segmentation, predictive analytics and graph analysis into operational workflows in order to provide immediate enhancements to business processes. This is becoming particularly useful as organisations move towards the real-time provisioning of goods and services. Furthermore, big data analytics is fuelling the IT and advertising industries, with up to a quarter of the $500 billion per year spent globally on advertising now being used to produce internet ads (*The Economist* 2014). Therefore, big data is providing great value to the commercial sector. However, that data is not openly available, which raises questions about how some players in the commercial sector, such as SMEs as well as government and other stakeholders, including citizens, can use this data.

The potential of big data for government and government departments is being discussed by public sector stakeholders. Although it is still unclear exactly how big data can be utilised by government, its potential value has been recognised. The opportunities and challenges of big data are also being explored by the European statistical agencies to see how, and to what extent, these new data sources can be incorporated into the production of official statistics (Eurostat Big Data Task Force 2014). The Communication: 'Towards a thriving data-driven economy' (EC 2014) is an important policy document, because it seeks to improve the ways in which the benefits of big data can be maximised. It focuses on enabling services and infrastructures with statistical infrastructures to play a strong role in a data-driven economy. Eurostat is also seeking to understand how big data sources can contribute to data-driven policymaking. With this in mind, a roadmap was adopted in September 2014 to provide guidance on key issues including policy, data sources, applications, methods, quality, infrastructure, skills, governance and legislation. The roadmap comprised a series of pilot studies focusing on data from mobile phones, websites, satellites, sensor networks and commercial or financial transactions, in order to understand how this data could be used in a reliable way. The pilots also meant that the private sector started to engage with policymakers to explore what kinds of data might be useful for public policy and research. This enabled discussions about which data could be shared and which might remain commercially sensitive. This is important because there is a need to find ways to respect commercial confidentiality (of the data provider) and personal confidentiality (of the data subject) in order to widen the social benefits. This is also significant in relation to the risks of big data applications in both the public and private sector, which result in negative social impacts around the way that personal data is being collected, processed and marketed.

For instance, Podesta *et al.* (2014) found that, although big data may be used for social good, it can also generate social harms or render outcomes that have inequitable impacts, even when discrimination is not intended. Small biases have the potential to become cumulative, affecting a wide range of consequences for certain disadvantaged groups. Podesta *et al.* (*Ibid.*) argue that steps must be taken to guard against such potential harms, by ensuring that power is appropriately balanced between individuals and institutions, whether between citizen and government, consumer and firm, or employee and business. They maintain in their recommendations that data should, therefore, be treated as a public resource.[4]

This suggestion relates to concerns about the shape of the digital market, which has been discussed by the European Parliament and Council by the European Data Protection Supervisor (EDPS). The EDPS (2014) points out that the vibrant growth of the digital marketplace is resulting in the concentration of a few overwhelming players and a resultant, increasing imbalance of power between big companies on the one hand, and SMEs and citizens on the other. It also notes that many ostensibly 'free' internet services are, in fact, paid for by the consumer by them surrendering their personal data. 'For many consumers, personal information operates as a currency and sometimes the only currency in the exchange for online services' (EDPS 2014, p. 10). The review shows that there are a number of legal and ethical issues at play in the social impact of big data, and these are found between data protection, competition law, and consumer protection (Chapter Eight discusses the range of legal and ethical issues in more detail).

Data protection legislation applies to organisations or businesses offering goods or services to individuals. A key part of this legislation is 'informed consent', which is one of the legal bases of data processing. This consent must be based on information provided *before* the data processing take place, and should be explained in clear and understandable language. However, many practices in the digital market risk violating these legal principles, because often consent is not requested in advance, particularly

---

4   The other recommendations are: developing frameworks for preserving privacy values; educating young people on how to use data whilst protecting their personal data; preventing discriminatory use of the data; and ensuring responsible use of big data by law enforcement and national security agencies.

by third-party data aggregators and, even when it is requested, the language used may be deliberately written in ways that only the most skilled legal individual can follow. Fair competition is one of the foundations of the EU single market, and its legal framework is set to guard against dominant positions that may distort the market becoming established. Such dominance involves having the ability to determine prices and control production, and abuses of a dominant position may include tying the consumer to specific services or bundling services inside packages that inhibit competitors from effectively entering the market.

These practices are increasingly common in the digital market, where 'free' offers of digital services encourage users to expand the applications they use on one platform, making the opportunity cost of changing provider very high. EU consumer protection law aims to remove barriers to the internal market, building trust in services on the basis of transparency and fairness. The latter applies, in particular, to the provision of clear information which enables consumers to make informed choices. Misleading practices include those in which a trader 'hides, or provides in an unclear, unintelligible, ambiguous or untimely manner information,' or when a product is described as 'free' or 'without charge' when, in effect, the consumer has to pay for it in other ways (for example surrendering personal information which is then traded without the user's informed knowledge or consent).

At the present time, these three key areas of EU law are handled independently and monitored by different authorities at the national level. The Data Protection Supervisor (2014) asserts that current developments in the digital market are exploiting the gap between technological advances, the legal framework and lack of coordination across legal domains. This is potentially causing harm to the consumer, reducing competition and consumer choice. The asymmetry of knowledge between a few service providers and most consumers is likely to increase as the Internet of Things develops. This is the way that embedded devices collect and share personal data without users knowing about the extent of such collection or being able to consult any documentation about it, including privacy statements.

In the digital economy, personal information represents a significant intangible asset in value creation as well as a currency in the exchange of online services. This has potentially far-reaching implications for the interpretation of key concepts including transparency, market dominance and consumer welfare and harm (*Ibid.*, p. 37). As a result of its review, the EDPS recommends developing a comprehensive response, including greater cooperation across policy areas and member states, to make the enforcement of competition and consumer protection rules more effective.

Big data as a new data source has the potential to enhance use of the data collected for official statistics. However, the ownership of big data is contested and, in many ways, it is more helpful to think about who controls the data, who can manipulate and use it. The data itself comes from users of digital products and services, and it is through their social relations and the technology used that big data is produced (Ruppert 2015). However, the ability to use that data is largely lodged with a range of commercial services and product developers. Given that big data is produced by users including citizens, there is a focus on government agencies engaging with the private sector, because the private sector now holds data that is potentially useful for public policy and research. However, as yet big data is not open across the commercial sector (see Chapter Nine) let alone for public use and may well be a barrier to the development of a genuinely open knowledge society, because it may well reduce consumer choice and harm citizens.

Provenance of data and data ecosystems

The discussion so far has highlighted the reality that data and developments of open data vary in relation to different sectors and kinds of data. The development of open data requires an infrastructure to support it and the provenance of data and its basic characteristics are important. The provenance of data rests with three main sectors: the public sector as in government and its related services, the private sector and its marketing services, and the research sector (Houghton 2014). Each of these sectors is comprised of institutions and organisations to create a data ecosystem, and each of these includes both dynamic and static data.

Dynamic data refers to data that are continually generated. Much public sector information is dynamic, as it is continually being produced as part of the functioning of government (e.g. national statistics, business registries, meteorological and geospatial data). These data are often readily usable in commercial applications with relatively little transformation of the raw data, as well as forming the basis for extensive elaboration. Much research data is dynamic, in the sense of being continually produced as a part of the research process, but it can also take the form of one-off project data or provide the basis of static collections. For example, site-based archaeological information may be the basis of a museum's collection (*Ibid.*). Static data refers to data that are part of an established record or collection, which may be held by public sector agencies, but may not have been created by them. Static data collections are typically the province of the galleries, libraries, archives, and museums sector (GLAM), although this mapping is not perfect, nor is the distinction between static and dynamic always entirely clear (*Ibid.*).

The potential of data and open data can only be realised if there is a structure and network in place to ensure that the data can be curated, stored and shared in an open manner. This requires the development of data ecosystems, which are comprised of a range of stakeholders, systems and data standards. Each area of data – research, government and big data – are currently developing their own ecosystems, and these emerging data ecosystems include differing social actors, economic, social and technological relationships. This raises the distinction between the key characteristics of data that is 'born digital' or that which has been digitised. These characteristics are significant because they facilitate particular ways of producing, circulating and sharing data across an ecosystem.

The term 'data ecosystem' was coined by O'Reilly in early discussions on open government (Harrison *et al.* 2012). Making government data open involves interacting with a range of stakeholders, as is the case for research data. Furthermore, in an open research data ecosystem, it is not a straightforward task to construct an OGD ecosystem. This requires identifying who the stakeholder groups are and creating appropriate business cases to encourage their usage. There are three categories of OGD ecosystems:

– Ecosystem of data producers: government data are produced by very different types of actors: e.g. public sector, academia, media and the private sector. As the relevance of linked data and data crowdsourcing increases in relation to value creation, the interactions between data producers and networks of data producers will become more complex.
– Ecosystem of infomediaries: as intermediate consumers of data, infomediaries (e.g. media developers, civil society) play an essential role in making sense of, and creating value out of raw data.
– Ecosystem of users: communities need to use data and engage with the data in order to get the most out of OGD. Libraries play a key role as a facilitator of data accessibility (*Ibid.*).

The research sector is also seeking to develop data ecosystems for research data. However, as yet, open research data within the research sector is still fragmented. Here, recommendations are still at the level of mobilising a stakeholder group to come together and discuss the issues (Tsoukala *et al.* 2015). In terms of big data, the private sector has created various types of ecosystems that enable them to harvest, mine and analyse data drawn from a range of data services, products and, increasingly, the Internet of Things.

Attention to the provenance and character of data is important in understanding the ways in which data ecosystems are emerging and can be developed. The development of ecosystems varies in their levels of openness. For example, some OGD ecosystems provide good exemplars amongst uneven provision, while academic research is slowly developing some open access ecosystems and big data ecosystems, although these are still lodged behind proprietary walls.

Conclusion

The creation and use of data is shaped by its context and rationale. Data is defined in very broad ways by scientific, policy and commercial research agencies and bodies, which provides the basis of defining open data or open works. Although data is widely defined, it is categorised by its community of producers and users. Thus, there are government data of various sorts, a vast array of scientific data, and big data. Government data and scientific data are primarily funded by public money and there is, therefore, a rationale for making that data open economically as well as socially. Although big data is not generally open, there is debate about data ownership, including what parts of that data should be shared with government departments, since citizens largely provide their data in return for convenience.

Although the way that data is defined is important, this chapter shows that the vision of open data is significant in relation to the shaping of data usage. Civil society actors, for example, envisage that open data can improve social life, while governments think that open data will improve the transparency of their decision making. Policymaking communities are urging the commercial sector to make some aspects of big data open, as this will counter unfair concentration in the digital marketplace and will ensure personal data privacy. These visions are still being debated by the actors concerned, but they underpin the ways in which social actors are seeking to mobilise open data. This means that data and its various types of characteristics are being created within specific ecosystems and contexts. The openness of those contexts varies, linked to aspirations for open data and the purposes which open data can be used for in society. Therefore, data and its visions of use are being mobilised to shape the development of a knowledge society, and its potential characteristics.

Given this, RECODE takes as its unit of analysis the data ecosystems related to five different disciplinary communities to understand how these data ecosystems function, who their members are and how they value the openness of data. In order to do so, the project examines some of the grand challenges for open government data, open research data and big data explored in this chapter, including stakeholder values and inter-relationships, technology barriers, legal and ethical considerations and institutional and policy issues. Using this information, both the project and this book provide insights into the ways in which the movement towards open data is producing tangible gains towards a knowledge society as well as the characteristics that are visible from this perspective.

4. Mobilising open data

Introduction

This chapter addresses the dynamics of the ways in which open data is being mobilised in society. The previous chapters noted how the position of scientific knowledge in wider social and economic life has changed in late modernity, and explained that data and open data are being discussed by governments and civil society organisations in ways that focus on the possible social benefits of open data. These two areas – the changing role of knowledge in society and the possible benefits of open data – should be viewed in relation to each other, because the aspirations for open data are often couched in terms of the role that knowledge plays in society. Furthermore, the possibility of open data, combined with changing senses of the position of knowledge, are utilised within various visions of a future, more knowledgeable society. Within these discussions, there is recognition of the potential benefits to society as well as an acknowledgement of what needs to be done to ensure that open data is produced and used in responsible ways. An overarching theme in these discourses is that of 'open' – both in terms of open data and open society.

To address the dynamics of mobilising open data, the chapter first outlines the various main ideas about what constitutes open, and the value of open as understood by open data advocates. Second, it identifies the ways in which open data advocates are working in relation to the characteristics of social movements. Given that the value of open is key idea or concept within notions of open data and open society, the next section considers of the value of open in knowledge production. The chapter then outlines the history of openness as part of WWW culture, before looking at the configuration of actors that are combining to create a movement for open data. Next, the chapter addresses the ways in which ordinary people can engage with data, and points out that the development of interpretive communities is important in making data useful for wider populations.

Summary of the overarching context of a movement pushing for open data

Advocates of open data – each having visions and values of open data – are organising themselves with the aim of mobilising open data in society. This mobilisation is based on their respective values and visions, which are not necessarily based on an explicit notion of a knowledge society, although they each work with ideas about a knowledgeable society. There is a wide range of understanding about what is meant by open, and how it might best be mobilised in data, in science, in knowledge production, and in society. Questions about what open means in science and in society have been debated historically and are re-emerging in relation to open data and knowledge society. The debates and visions many well inform change; however, as Stehr (1994) notes, the transition to a knowledge society is not being achieved in any planned or coherent manner; rather, the realisation of a knowledge society is occurring through an array of actions in relation to various uncoordinated institutional frameworks. They are linked through various types of social mobilisations that are clustering around the theme of open in relation to data, and all relate to ideas about open science and open society. As the previous chapter explained, government policymakers and civil society organisations are seeking to develop open data. Although the policy push is a key feature in mobilising open data, civil society organisations are a strong mobilising force. They play a key role by acting as a data movement and, to some extent, a social movement. Social movements are instrumental in shaping the discourses around causes, in bringing people together to push for change, and in connecting policy sensibilities with public sensibilities. This is important because, in order for open data to produce the transformation into a knowledge society, citizens using data in their daily lives must be involved, just as much as knowledge producers and government services. This discussion links explicitly with RECODE because of the ways in which scientists and other stakeholders, who are often outside the open data movement, must be mobilised in order to achieve the policy and civil society goals of a knowledge society.

Understanding the mobilisation of open data as a movement

In general terms, the concept of a social movement is rooted in theories that seek to address various forms of collective action.[1] Although there is debate about different types of social movement, the 'new social movement

---

1   There are several approaches within the study of social movements, such as political process theory, and resource mobilisation theory.

theory'[2] – in the context of Castells' (2001) digital networked society – provides a lens through which we can understand the ways that social movements are operating in the context of open data. A distinctive feature of contemporary social movements is that they involve a 'lifeworld' focus, where debate and communication serve to create a normative consensus (Habermas 1984, 1987). In part, this is a reaction to the fact that economic and political institutions are increasingly interfering in lifeworlds. These intrusions generate responses that are organised though social movements based around issues such as quality of life, democratic participation and identity (Staggenborg 2011). Although the focus on culture is often seen as distinct from structure, Polletta (2004) argues that these need not mutually exclusive. Rather, when culture is understood as 'the symbolic dimensions of all structures, institutions and practices' (*Ibid.*, p. 100), then social movements are engaging with both structural and cultural issues. This focus means that social movements in contemporary society can be defined as 'purposive collective actions aiming at the transformations of values and institutions of society' (Castells 2001, p. 138). Open data spans across both cultural and structural areas of contemporary society because knowledge both structures social life and is culturally shaped by social relations.

Another feature of contemporary social movements is that they use the flexibility of the WWW to organise action and often manifest themselves via digital platforms and networks (Castells, 2001). Given this context, Melucci (1996) argues that social movements are no longer collections of relatively stable organisations, or even unified actors, but instead are often fluid networks that can foster collective action as and when needed. Social movements can then be characterised by their fluidity and flexibility as well as their focus on particular issues or values that might be distributed across networks. Melucci (1988) writes that, 'to understand the way social movements are constructed requires looking at the formation and maintenance of the cognitive frameworks and social relationships that form the basis of collective action' (*Ibid.*, p. 331).

The dynamics of these movements means that relationships are often formed within submerged networks in which new collective identities

2   There is some debate that questions whether there really is a 'new' social movement theory, because some of the issues, such as labour, predate post-industrial and information society issues (Cohen and Rai 2000). Nonetheless, commentators such as Klandermans (1986) argue that new movements are emerging from a range of issues and grievances rooted in post-industrial society and in information society developments. Examples of these include the peace movement, the environmental movement, and the women's movement.

or identifications with an issue are formed. From this type of activity, activists generate new cultural models and symbolic challenges (Mueller 1994, pp. 247–248). Activists' perceptions of, belief in and emotions towards the cause, along with their adherence to a set of values, all play into the way that social movements emerge and act (Staggenborg 2011). Developing and framing an issue or issues under question involves interaction and mobilisation, which occurs through particular episodes of contention. This leads McAdam *et al.* (2001) to assert that attention needs to be paid to how actors attribute threats and opportunities, how they appropriate mobilising structures, construct frames and meanings, and innovate collective action tactics.

An analysis of the way that civil society organisations frame open data and build networks reveals a striking similarity to the way that social movements work (see Chapter Three). For example, activists lobbying for open data are seeking to mobilise large-scale changes and working across everyday networks of personal contacts as well as organisational structures of data producers and providers. There is also some indication of a collective identity emerging across the various networks that are pushing for open data. Currently, this identity is not highly formalised but is, nonetheless, recognised as people who are 'pro' open data, whether in research, government or civil society contexts. Some aspects of the networks are to some degree submerged, such as the work of repositories and data archives. There is also a drive to develop new ways to support open data, such as ecosystems, new institutional guidelines and new data practices. These types of activities are advocating a whole new set of values around data: in particular, proposing that data should no longer be owned by any one institution or person, but be publicly-owned instead. Furthermore, some new constituents in the ecosystem are emerging, in terms of institutional relations, new data curation services and new types of expertise and practice, such as data management plans, which have to be managed and implemented by those who may be outside the recognised social movement. These developments are part of the way that civil society organisations are pressing for open data, but they will only be accomplished if those other stakeholders are successfully motivated and mobilised. This mobilisation is also built on an ideology of openness that is a distinctive feature of early digital culture. Even if this has been partially undermined through the commercialisation of the WWW, openness still remains a defining feature of digital culture.

Openness as a value: Society, science and the World Wide Web (WWW)

When discussing open data, it is important to understand what is meant by open – not only in relation to data, but also in relation to knowledge production and society. There are many uses of open and openness, which are often related to notions of freedom and what is free. Open can refer to open society as well as the way that open is practised in a range of areas, such as free speech and free software. This notion of open is also used in expressions about freedom, such as freedom of expression, freedom of the press and freedom of movement. These are expressions of aspects of open society and the ways in which open society is negotiated. The notion of open is important in assessing the way that open data and open science or knowledge production are related in transforming society into a knowledge society which, in its idealistic sense, creates an open society.

Debates about open society were being held as long ago as the world of classical Athens where, for example, Pericles spoke out in favour of an open society. Pericles called for a society in which citizens were equal before the law and had influence in society (Brin 1998). However, this early vision was soon crushed after the Peloponnesian War (431–403 BC), and Plato later questioned the wisdom of having an open society and democracy (Popper 1966). The influence of Plato and his followers meant that the idea of an open and free society was not being advocated until the philosophical work of Locke during the Enlightenment, which was then developed in America by politicians Jefferson and Madison. These early notions of an open society were not, however, inclusive societies, as they incorporated slavery and colonialism, which had political structures that generated oppression and imprisonment for some against the rights and freedoms of others. Reflecting on Nazism and Stalinism, Popper (1966) explores the way that Plato's hatred of empiricism and democracy flowed through into Hegel's ideals, then onto Nazi officers and Marxist-Leninist commissars. Attempts to overthrow these oppressive regimes, from the 1940s to the fall of the Berlin Wall in 1989, resulted in a period where the idea and reality of freedom seemed to hang in the balance.

Popper (1966) highlights that notion that open society is fragile. Writers such as Orwell and Huxley addressed the ways that new technologies, surveillance and management programmes threatened open society. The struggle for open society continues today, and is on a global scale – in both old and new ways. Thus, slavery still exists in some forms, whereas digital technology closely monitors individuals within a surveillance society. The debate about what open society might mean in a digital context is once more raising concerns about freedom and democracy. In this context, freedom is debated in terms of who has what knowledge and the belief that there needs to be a transparency about what knowledge actors have of each other. In the popular writings of David Brin (1999), this is termed as working towards a 'transparent society'.

This brief overview provides some evidence that the notion of open, and its related concept of freedom, has a long history with a broad application. In science, open is mostly used in debates about open science within the institution, as well as being part of wider society. Chapter Two showed how science is embedded in social relations, negotiating what open means for its work and considering how it relates to society more broadly. If we take science to mean the systematic pursuit of knowledge, then it plays a role in making the world knowable. As Chapter Two outlined, the position and role of science is changing, in line with changes in society, and is doing so both philosophically and empirically. Fuller (1999) notes that science as the pursuit of knowledge underwent a range of changes during the twentieth century. However, even including shifts such as Mode 2 knowledge production, Fuller stresses that the political rhetoric which positions science in society remains largely unchanged. He writes that science is still governed by a self-selecting group who decide who can qualify as scientists through examinations and by determining what is deemed to count as knowledge, through publication strategies. The position of science and its authority as a self-regulatory institution is a generally-accepted normative one. Even when cases of research fraud are discovered by the research community, these are seen to validate the critical stance in science. Science's authority means that it is listened to by policymakers, industry and ordinary people who not may fully understand the science, which, in reverse, means that scientists may not fully understand the context in which science is applied. This 'mutually tolerable ignorance' is something that is established and accepted (Fuller 1999).

A knowledge society is partly based on this normative position of science, with an assumption in the normative ideal that science is an open community. Although imperfectly realised, the ideal of the open society of science remains dominant in policy areas. This links with Steve Fuller's argument for what he terms a 'welfare economics of science' or 'knowledge policy' that will ensure equal and informed access to data and knowledge (Fuller 1988, 1993, 1997). Fuller's argument for an open science is shaped by republican values, as espoused by Popper's stance on open society. A republic of science or open science seeks to position itself between the excesses of communitarian and liberal approaches within a society-science relationship. For example, societies with a strong communitarian ethos may censor research that could be used in negative ways in policy, such as the possibility of creating a 'racial science that could be used to develop a political movement like Nazism' (Fuller 1999, p. 12). In terms of liberal societies, there is a threat to the integrity of science in the way that market values intervene in free inquiry. In this context, free market and free inquiry are seen as the same thing, so any research can be undertaken as long as there is sufficient money to do it. Given that the cost of research is high across the range of disciplines, there is a tendency for research that attracts funding to develop, which may result in some areas of study being under-investigated. This may lead some researchers to seek funding from private investors for their work. There is also a lack of questioning the value of some well-funded research programmes, such as high-energy physics. These are the types of issues arising from the way in which 'science functions in society and this impacts on what kind of knowledge is produced, as well as how such knowledge may be used' (*Ibid.*, p. 13).

To ensure that science can act as open science and as a republic of science, some basic conditions must be met which relate to the practice of science itself and to the ways that science and scientific knowledge acts in broader society. The conditions that underpin open science are that:
- People's opinions might change for the better as a result of hearing opposing opinions.
- People need not fear the consequences of their expressed opinions on their material well-being.
- There is a 'public good' or 'civic ideal' to which people may appeal in deliberation, which transcends specific individual and group interests (*Ibid.*, p. 15).

If republican science policies is the ideal, then those policies will seek to make sure that everyone is materially secure enough feel confident in expressing their own opinions. Here, Fuller notes (drawing on Popper) that, if someone can express their thoughts with impunity, then his or her ideas can be judged by others in an open way (*Ibid.*). This is significant because it highlights the importance of being able to speak out. This is not always an easy thing to do, and research has shown that, even in open contexts, many people still feel deferential to a hierarchical order or they may fear humiliation (Elster 1993), both of which will deter them from stating their opinions. Therefore, both material and psychological conditions have to be met so that science can function in an open way.

Another factor in making science open is the strength of a civic ideal and/or public good and the ways that they are understood. To be able to address different interests in society, there needs to be some overarching body or set of principles that can assess the impact of one set of interests on wider society (Fuller 1999). The notion of special interests assumes that there is some established civic ideal against which different arguments and developments can be debated in terms of a public good. In this way, special interests within a larger collective are valued – not in their own right – but only valued by the extent they can contribute to the wider population. This is different to intellectual property, which seeks to protect informa-tion owners being forced to make their data freely available. Fuller (*Ibid.*) argues that this is how the epistemological distinction between pure and applied knowledge is transformed into an economic choice between public good versus intellectual property. There is also an internal assumption of a commons within science, which is seen in the way in which scholars do not question scientific theory by using reasoning and data from another field, discipline or sub-discipline outside their own. If a scholar does want to challenge these norms as well as any scientific principles, then they need to propose their new ideas openly, so that they can be publicly scrutinised. Fuller (*Ibid.*) argues that the concept of a civil ideal and public good gener-ates an external boundary to the political and scientific endeavour. This enables internal changes to be followed, noted and questioned, and these types of processes create scientific conventions (Popper) or paradigms (Kuhn).

These processes are in play within the social relations of science that have political and economic influences internally on science as well as externally on wider society. This is significant because it affects what kind of knowledge is produced, the way that knowledge is produced and how knowledge is shared within wider society. Given that the normative idea of science still has authority and that knowledge society is based on ideas about the role of data in society, then the way that science functions affects how knowledge is produced and shared. Theorists of science such as Fuller (1999) assert that there are different models of science – some more open than others – which shape the possibilities of realising open science. Underpinning this, Fuller argues, is the principle of 'the right to be wrong' (*Ibid.*, p. 4). Therefore, in considering open data and the various open data movements and perspectives, it is necessary to ascertain if the material conditions are there to support openness. This means ensuring that scholars, scientists, policymakers and citizens have the right to be wrong and that there are sufficient checks and balances in both the production of knowledge and the use of knowledge. As this discussion shows, openness in science takes a particular form based on the mores of scientific communities and the ways that science is practiced. Furthermore, the ways in which science interacts with society also shapes the way that research data can be made publicly available. Thus, a cultural change in the practice of science will be required to make scientific data open (see Chapter Six for more detail on this).

The development of open data and open science is partly being enabled by digital technology, with some ideas about open and notions of freedom being inherent. Berners-Lee, the inventor of the WWW, brought together hypertext and the internet to build the WWW, and CERN released the first browser over the internet in August 1991. Berners-Lee argues that, throughout the Web's history, there have been parallels between technical design and social principles (Berners-Lee 1999). He designed the Web on universalistic (with lower case u) principles, to build an environment that would enable people to think and discuss diverse issues from a range of perspectives in an open and accepting way. This informed the development of decentralised systems of computers, knowledge, and people. Berners-Lee's values provide a narrative that focuses on the forms of participation in the WWW, in which:

> hope in life comes from the interconnections among all the people in the world. We believe that if we work for what we think individually is good then we as a whole will achieve more power, more understanding, more harmony as we continue the journey. We don't find the individual being subjugated by the whole. We don't find the needs of the whole being subjugated by the increasing power of the individual. But we might see more understanding in the struggles between these extremes (*Ibid.*, p. 228).

Berners-Lee (1999) understands freedom of the internet in two ways. First, freedom is experienced in terms of sending any content anywhere in the network in packets. Second, it provides a freedom of association which is based on mutual respect with an ethos of collective endeavour that goes beyond singular individual effort to build for the common good in ways that are unconstrained by bureaucratic regimes. This vision informed virtual communitarians who sought to use it to generate egalitarian and alternative communities. Their culture generated a context in which the internet moved beyond its specialist employment to more general social use. Thus, those early users of networked computing outside of university or hacker environments created virtual communities, using the term popularised by Rheingold (1993).

Castells (2001) notes that these communitarians contributed to the shape and evolution of the internet, including its commercial manifestations in decisive ways – for example, the earliest Bulletin Board Services (BBS) in the San Francisco Bay area and the work of the Institute for Global Communication (IGC) – focused on socially-responsible agendas such as protecting the environment and preserving world peace. IGC established the first women's computer network (La Neta), which was used by the Mexican Zapatistas to build international solidarity on behalf of 'Indian Communities'. Other community networks, like Schuler's Seattle Community Network or the Digital City Amsterdam, sought to renew or enhance citizen participation. Another historically specific use of internet-based networks was the way that Russian academics used it to organise activities for democracy and freedom during the perestroika period of dismantling the Soviet Union.

The history of the internet and WWW is tightly related to a range of open movements in social terms, which are based on the WWW's open architecture – including open source, open hardware and open content. The open data movement forms part of this overall open movement ethos. The distinctive feature of the open data movement is that it focuses on data, asserting that data should be freely available for reuse and republishing. As noted in Chapter Three, the overall drive and movement itself is made up of a variety of groups with a range of data-related backgrounds, which are self-organising and aim to promote and facilitate open data. A range of civil society movements are involved, such as the Open Data Foundation (ODF) and the Open Government Group (OGG). This push for open data is fully supported by Tim Berners-Lee, who is calling for 'raw data now'. He explains that he has moved from an initial focus on openly sharing documents to believing in the need to share raw data. Berners-Lee (2012) says that the open data movement's position focuses on how open data can interconnect and join data to summarise and compare, to monitor, extrapolate and infer.

Open in this context focuses on how open data interplays with knowledge generation and how this can be facilitated by the promotion of a robust commons that will enable anyone to participate. There are practical aspects to realising this vision, which include maximising interoperability to cover a wide range of data, systems and licences. The ODF expresses this by advocating that 'knowledge is open if anyone is free to access, use, modify, and share it – subject, at most, to measures that preserve provenance and openness.' As noted previously, the ODF argues that this core meaning of open data matches the open source definition used in software, and is synonymous with 'free' or 'libre' as defined by Free Cultural Works (https://creativecommons.org/freeworks/). The ODF's definition of open data was initially derived from the open source definition, which in turn was derived from the Debian Free Software Guidelines. Given this background, the term 'open data' as defined by ODF is used to denote the item or piece of knowledge being transferred. There is a level of regulation about this use, which is mainly operated through licences, as discussed in Chapter Three.

The configuration of an open data movement: The characteristics of social movements and actors in mobilising open data

As Chapter Three outlined, a range of organisations are actively promoting open data. There is also a strong push towards open data from governments and global regional actors such as the G8's Open Data Charter (https://www.gov.uk/government/publications/open-data-charter), the United Kingdom's open government data agenda (data.gov.uk), the United States' open data agenda (www.data.gov), the EU's open access to research data policy (EC 2016) and the OECD's Open Government Data project (OECD 2016). The G8, for instance, has high hopes for how data can be used in society and how open data could mobilise a knowledge society. It sees open data as an un-tapped resource with huge potential to encourage the building of stronger, more interconnected societies that better meet the needs of their citizens and allow innovation and prosperity to flourish. To foster the development of open data, the G8 has agreed to follow a set of principles that will provide a foundation for access to, and the release and reuse of data made available by G8 governments (see Chapter Three). The UK and US open government data initiatives are similar in that they focus on the ways in which open data can benefit citizens generally as well as finding new ways to facilitate innovation in both commercial and non-commercial settings. The G8 (representing many governments) recognises how important diversity is for stimulating creativity and innovation, believing that the more people and organisations use data, the greater social and economic benefits will be generated – again, for both commercial and non-commercial uses.

The basis of this type of action is a vision of open data that is largely based on a range of civil society organisations. The open data movement is rooted in the culture of freedom and openness that is at the heart of WWW culture. This continues today with Tim Berners-Lee still campaigning and now pushing for open raw data. This momentum and drive for change is also enacted by the civil society organisations which are seeking to mobilise open data. These organisations often comprise elements of social movements in that they are framing the debate and agenda, they are garnering support from a range of actors, and they are articulating the opening up of data in both cultural and structural terms. They are addressing the cultural issues around opening up data by focusing on perceptions of how data should be shared and on the practices for sharing data. They are also addressing structural issues by pushing for institutional change to support open data as well as detailed changes at the institutional level, for instance, the legal, regulatory and ethical aspects of data. Each of these are relevant for all types of open data, including open research data, and form the 'grand challenges' that were examined within the RECODE project and presented in more detail in Chapters Five to Nine.

Although there is a common focus, the movement for open data is made up of a number of advocates based in civil society. There are different groups with varying foci and perspectives. As well as the key actors mentioned in Chapter Three, these include the Open Data Institute, the World Wide Web Foundation, the World Wide Web Consortium (W3C), the 'Web We Want', and the Open Data Research Network. All of these organisations are addressing open data and, although each considers open data in general terms, each organisation also considers how open data can be used in various aspects of social life. The 'Web Index', an organisation within the World Wide Web Foundation, focuses on measuring the Web's contribution to development and human rights at the global level.

Part of the way that open data advocates are working and joining together to make an open data movement is lodged in their respective focus on how to make data open, each arguing that a range of technical, institutional, legal and social factors need to be addressed in order to operationalise open data. This aim is based on a range of sub-themes, which inform and underpin the requirement of what is termed 'open works' or open data. To support the responsible sharing of data and making data open, one actor, the ODF, created sub-themes seeking to facilitate the distribution of open works. The sub-themes include open licensing, as ODF, in line with other open data advocates, asserts that open data must be available under an open licence and that any additional conditions accompanying the work (such as terms of use, or patents held by the licensor) must not contradict the terms of the licence (see Chapter Eight for a full discussion on this).

As Chapter Three discussed, open licences include a range of conditions and permissions that are based on key sub-themes found in the open data movement. These include free use and redistribution of the licenced work, including sale – whether on its own or as part of a collection made from works from different sources. The theme of modification is also evident in licences, as are the creation of derivatives and the distribution of such derivatives. Another sub-theme is the demand that data should be available to be freely used, distributed, or modified separately from any other part of the work or from any collection of works in which it was originally distributed. The sub-theme of compilation also focuses on distribution, pointing out that open data can be used alongside other distinct works without placing restrictions on these other works. One major sub-theme is the belief that open data should be based on a non-discriminatory agenda, in that licences and general accessibility must not discriminate against any person or group. Attribution is another important sub-theme, insisting that open data users should give credit to the contributors, rights holders, sponsors and creators.

A further sub-theme addresses the issue of access, which states that open works and open data should be available as a whole and at a reasonable one-time reproduction cost, preferably downloadable via the internet without charge. Part of the accessibility sub-theme is that open data should be provided in open format, which means that the data must be provided in a convenient and modifiable form to ensure that there are no unnecessary technological obstacles to people trying to exercise the licensed rights. Specifically, data should be machine-readable, available in bulk, and provided in an open format (i.e. a format with a freely-available published specification which ensures there is no restriction – monetary or otherwise – on its use) or, at the very least, can be processed using just one free/libre/open-source software tool.

The way in which the various actors are operating in the push to mobilise open data is based on their definitions of open data. Chapter Three discussed various definitions of open data, the principles of those definitions, and the ways that open data can be used in practical terms. Social movements around open data operate in a similar way to that of others, in that several organisations each have a distinctive focus, but act together under the umbrella of open data to mobilise open data across many social areas. Thus, for example, OGD focuses on government data, ODF looks across a range of data but focuses on developing training for citizens, and the EU is pushing the commercial sector to open up big data.

These policy and civil society actors are working in the same mobilising space so, in that sense, are forming a social movement. The combination of these actors is acting as a network among particular domains of data, social constituencies and contexts to mobilise open data in wider society. The key principle of open data unites the distinctive actors, with each acting in relation to their respective social constituencies to bring about change. This collaborative action is generating the conditions for data to contribute to a transformation to a knowledge society.

Open data in wider society: Citizens and organisations access and use of data

Although open data movements are seeking to develop open data, there is still the question of how ordinary people and organisations (public, private and third sector) can access and engage with open data. In order to mobilise change towards knowledge society, data literacy needs to improve across the population. It also requires an awareness and better understanding amongst people and organisations of how to unlock the value of open data. This involves education about data literacy and ways to interpret and use data as well as fostering good practice by providing data in machine-readable formats to empower a future generation of data innovators. The commercial sector is focusing its attention on how to realise the value of open data. In the US, for instance, the Chamber of Commerce Foundation is working with New York University's Governance Lab to explore how the value of open data can be realised in the commercial sector (see Chapter Nine). The attention in this context is on data-driven innovation, seeking to understand how open data and big data can be used for innovation (US Chamber of Commerce Foundation 2014).

In board terms, the US Chamber of Commerce argues that four kinds of open data drive innovation: scientific, social, personal, and governmental. There is an assumption that researchers work collaboratively with scientific data and that this is driving forward knowledge in scientific terms. In the commercial sector, businesses and other organisations use social data from blogs, company reviews, and social media posts to obtain consumer opinions on products, services and brands. There is general recognition that the public sector provides the most robust open data, as shown by examples such as the US Food and Drug Administration (FDA)'s 'OpenFDA' portal, which allows anyone access to publicly-available FDA data. In social terms, the US Chamber of Commerce argues, new digital applications are giving citizens access to their own personal data, therefore yielding more informed consumers. The focus here is on enabling people to be data consumers, so it does not extend to considering how they can add value to, or improve their lives by data. Furthermore, there is little attention given to how they might utilise the value of the data they produce through social media and other data sources that harvest consumer data. Here issues of privacy are important, as discussed in Chapter Eight.

The use of open data by ordinary people is still relatively low (Cornford *et al.* 2013). In general, people without a technical background are most usually what can be termed 'data consumers'. Individuals mainly use applications that make data accessible for data consumers and rarely, if ever, use raw data. Even if individuals get involved in open data projects where they can develop new skills, they tend to rely on intermediaries such as programmers and data integrators to help them access data. The activities individuals carry out depends on which technological skills they already have. Ordinary data users include programmers, data integrators, citizens, champions, facilitators and open data advocates (Hivan and Titah 2015). These types of users often perform more than one activity, so they need to collaborate because the work is too big and complex to be done by one person. According to Hivan and Titah (*Ibid.*), there are five activities that give data value: (1) identifying data; (2) requesting data; (3) converting data; 4) programming; and 5) promoting data. Hivan and Titah's study (*Ibid.*) of open data projects in Montréal, Canada shows that these activities are identified and allocated to people through planning days which identify projects and bring citizens together to create a team. Once this stage is reached, a project has a champion designed to be a public supporter of the project (*Ibid.*).

In the context of resident-supported open data projects in cities, open data advocacy groups help to promote the applications devised for citizen's use. These groups devise open data projects that they hope will convince a city to pursue its efforts towards open data programmes and will develop an open culture within local government. A critical dimension of open data projects is assigning responsibilities to individuals to cover all the activities involved. It is important that individuals have a feeling of ownership and of actively facilitating change, because this motivates them to take part and to see the value of using data. One example is an anti-corruption hackathon that was held in Québec (Rocha 2012). Here, instead of simply complaining about corruption, individuals recruited programmers, journalists, civil society groups and other city residents to challenge the misconduct using data. The project used data to spot links and patterns between calls for public tenders and contracts awarded to specific organisations by the City of Montréal.

An important factor in enabling city residents to use open data is the design of data portals. An easy-to-use portal encourages data use and this has been identified as an important dimension in explaining the use of data by individuals. Hivan and Titah (2015) found that Montréal's data portal is easier to use than many others. The participants in their study said that they found the portals from Boston, Toronto and New York less easy to use, and that they got lost when searching data sets. The complexity of accessing and interrogating data is a constraint on data use. In order to use data, a user must have a level of data literacy and the capacity to collect, treat, analyse, and communicate with large quantity of data. In Hivan and Titah's (*Ibid.*) study in Canada, the participants thought that city councils should be responsible for providing data literacy education for their citizens. One open data advocate in Montréal argued that data literacy is an important issue in terms of participation, because it is part of deepening an informed participation. Evidence from open data projects, such as those by Hivan and Titah in Montréal, shows that providing data literacy and easy-to-use portals are important in an open data ecosystem. Another dimension of enabling genuine participation in using data is the level of citizens' inclusiveness. Here, Berry (2008), for example, distinguishes between the image of open source information as a 'commons', and the reality, which is often that of a 'club good' enjoyed by restricted group of people who have the necessary data and technical skills to analyse and interpret the data. This point also relates to big data, as Boyd and Crawford (2012) and Carlson and Anderson (2007) note. The use of open data for social transformation towards an inclusive knowledge society therefore needs to be placed in the wider context of inclusive and interpretative communities.

Therefore, although Hivan and Titah (2015) identify ways to facilitate ordinary people to use open data, there is also a need to address the ways in which these individuals may – or may not – form into interpretive communities (Cornford *et al.* 2015). There is a strong focus by actors in the open data movement on practical aspects such as licensing, open artefacts and education, however little attention is paid to the data interpretation. As Davies and Bawa (2012) assert, openness needs to be seen as a process that is rooted in communities. They argue that this does not just depend on the open artefacts within communities, but on how they support their members' interpretive skills. Interpretative communities can be understood as 'reference groups', whose perspective provides a frame of reference for individuals within the group (Shubutani 1955). Interpretive communities also contribute towards the social production of knowledge, including formal knowledge. As Chapters Two and Three noted, it is now a well-established fact that scientific knowledge, as well as other forms of knowledge, is created by communities (Porter 1995). Communities produce a range of forms of knowledge and define the types and the qualities of the knowledge they produce. This point leads to the consideration of interpretation – because the production of knowledge and the use of knowledge requires interpretation. The framing of interpretation occurs within communities – the cultures of communities shape the way that artefacts and symbolic goods become knowable. As Fish suggests, 'there is no single way of reading that is correct or natural, only 'ways of reading' that are extensions of community perspectives' (Fish 1980, p. 16). He argues that 'interpretation is the source of texts, facts, authors and intentions' (*Ibid.*, p. 16) and we add data to this. Fish develops this idea further by saying that these entities (in which we include data), which 'were once seen as competing for the right to constrain interpretation (text, reader, author) are now all seen to be the products of interpretation' (*Ibid.*, pp. 16–17). Therefore, for open data to be transformative, there need to be interpretive communities within society.

However, Cornford *et al.* (2015) argue that UK developments in open data have not reached their full potential, because insufficient attention has been focused on supporting the development of interpretive communities. Despite work by open government advocates in the UK, the current situation means that individuals tend only to be able to act as 'armchair auditors' in using open data, because of the lack of interpretive communities. Cornford *et al.* (*Ibid.*) point out that there need to be more opportunities for individuals to act effectively with data. In the first instance, this requires help from intermediary organisations which are capable of processing data and can support the interpretation of data. The learning gained from these intermediary organisations may then foster community learning, enabling individuals to gain the relevant expertise as part of an interpretive community, as open data-based participation. Cornford *et al.* (*Ibid.*) argue that support is needed to grow interpretive communities, which requires the development of an institutional context for citizen and individual engagement in the interpretation of data. This involves a move from a primary focus on openness in mechanistic terms to one that also addresses process (Joshi and Houtzager 2012). In order to use open data to transform to an open knowledge society, the social and political processes are important for ensuring that accountability within knowledge production is rooted in citizens and individuals, rather than elite governing bodies. Therefore, as Worthy (2012) argues, the development of open data within an open society framework needs to be embedded within communities – whether communities of place, interest or association – that enables the interpretation of data. Furthermore, these communities need to devise governance processes to ensure accountability for the responsible use of data. As such, the disciplinary practices examined within RECODE as well as the stakeholder practices and inter-relationships within them, provide valuable evidence about these processes within a particular open data use case. The information gained within RECODE will provide some pathways for further development of this sector to assist in enabling these practices to develop in responsible ways.

Conclusion

The main themes of the open data movement are the value placed on 'openness' and the ways that open data can be a key driver of change, towards open science and open society as well as data-driven commercial innovation. Those in the open data movement are convinced that open data has the potential to be valuable for society, in both general and specific terms. There is a consensus about the value of open data across a wide range of social and economic life, such as open government, development and human rights, innovation and commerce. In order to mobilise open data actors within the wide remit of the open data movement, there is a need to develop protocols for open data use, easy-to-use open data portals and, as some activists urge, the development of data literacy. Realising the aspirations for open data, open society and open science is complex and it requires technological, institutional, and legal change to be embedded within the social change of achieving a knowledge society. Any transformation in developing a knowledge society using open data rests on the characteristics of the social production of knowledge. This requires citizens and organisations to have the necessary skills and time to use data in a knowledgeable way, and in ways that transform social life in a democratic and accountable way. Importantly, this means addressing the process of open data and finding ways to create and sustain interpretive communities, where there is a right to be wrong and a data welfare system. This last point is important because open data has the potential to create a participative open society – however, it can also fragment and create fragility in society. Once an openly accountable process of open data is in place, bringing open technology and interpretive communities together, then open data can play a defining role in the mobilisation of a knowledge society.

RECODE represents one of the first empirical investigations of the mobilisation of open data. The lessons learned within the project provide some information about how activists, stakeholders and reluctant members of the community are engaging with open data practices and imperatives. In addition, it provides an opportunity to evaluate policy and practice in one sector to inform the development of these across all of the open data paradigms (open government data, open research data, big data and others). In Chapters Five to Nine, we examine some specific grand challenges – values and inter-relationships (Chapter Five), institutional practices (Chapter Six) and legal and ethical solutions (Chapter Eight) – case studies (geospatial data – Chapter Seven) and future directions (Chapter Nine) for managing open access to research data. These lessons will enable an evaluation of the progress towards, and characteristics of, an emerging knowledge society based on the availability and openness of data from governments, researchers, individuals and commercial organisations.

5. Institutions in the data ecosystem

Actors in the public knowledge domain and in private data companies[1]

Introduction

The role institutions play in mobilising open data and their position in that mobilisation are key aspects in the development of open data. As the discussion in Chapter Four shows, institutions act in response to the drivers that are pushing for open data and they are key actors in overseeing and implementing a range of changes to facilitate the development of open data. Institutions are also situated within other broader changes that affect how they operate, which include the significant changes in systems for generating, sharing, and disputing human knowledge using digital technologies (Edwards *et al.* 2011). As outlined in Chapter Two, the way knowledge is generated has changed over historical time and the shift to Mode 2 Knowledge Production means that it is now becoming an increasingly large-scale, global, interdisciplinary, collaborative effort organised around open data sharing. Part of that change is the way digital technologies, including formal university and research centre systems as well as open public systems and platforms such as social media, crowd-based knowledge phenomenon such as Wikipedia as well as big data, have enabled new ways of producing and circulating 'knowledge'. In general terms, this includes shifting to less-centralised forms of knowledge production and circulation. This has had an effect on the ecosystem and the way that institutions interrelate.

However, the move towards open data, in particular, is changing wider organisational processes of data production, dissemination and use. This change is key in defining and shaping any broader social change towards a knowledge society. The possibility of unrestricted availability of data makes possible new kinds of education, services, business models and scientific and scholarly communication practices. Institutions in the scientific and scholarly domain, such as libraries, data centres, national archives and universities, are expected to play a leading role in enabling these changes, by

---

1   This chapter draws on the RECODE report: *Institutional Barriers and Good Practice Solutions* (Noorman *et al.* 2014), http://recodeproject.eu/wp-content/uploads/2014/09/RECODE-D4.1-Institutional-barriers-FINAL.pdf.

developing and maintaining technical and organisational infrastructures for the production, preservation and sharing of open data. At the same time, these institutions are confronted with a rapidly-changing environment, in which relations between institutions within the data ecosystem are being continuously redefined. For many institutions, this is a relatively new and unchartered area, and most institutions have only taken initial steps in exploring and giving shape to their new roles and responsibilities.

This chapter moves beyond broad discussions about societal changes to focus on institutions that are involved in scientific and scholarly practices. It explores some of the changes that these institutions are undergoing and the resulting challenges they face. The next section examines the changes in the landscape, which is followed by a discussion of three institutional challenges in particular: securing funding for open access, controlling the quality of data, and providing training and education. The final section concludes by discussing how many institutions in this domain are renegotiating and reinventing their roles, responsibilities and relationships to position themselves as coordinating actors within the evolving data ecosystems. However, in order to successfully make data open, they need to engage meaningfully with research communities.

Institutions and their changing role in data ecosystems

As the previous chapters have shown, the move to making research data open is partly the result of a drive from a range of open data advocates and some level of top-down push for open access from policymakers. Institutions are therefore facing increasing demands from civil society organisations, policymakers and from scientific communities for access to data as well as data services and support. This section examines the ways that various actors envision how institutions and organisations may adjust to open data. In particular, it uses documentary evidence, including policy reports, strategy documents, and other relevant literature, from the institutional issues grand challenge research within the RECODE project to illuminate current negotiations about the changing role of institutions within the open access to research data ecosystem.

All the different activities required to make and keep data openly accessible take place within a network of institutions. The discussion in Chapter Three points to the different requirements that need to be put in place to make data open and that this requires considerable work to make data easy to access, use, and evaluate. Data must be digitally generated or converted into standardised and machine-readable formats and metadata must be added; the data and metadata have to be reviewed and checked for inconsistencies, noise or errors and, if possible, linked to other data sets. To store data and make them accessible, infrastructures must be funded, built, and maintained. As discussed in more detail in Chapters Six and Seven, tools must be developed to make the data searchable and reusable. To preserve the quality of data, multiple versions of data sets have to be managed and occasionally migrated to other, new technological platforms. Furthermore, the general requirements of making data open as outlined in Chapter Three and as the issues of doing so at the research practice level as discussed in Chapters Six, Seven and Eight, including copyright issues and informed consent, must also be clarified and managed. Additionally, making research data available for unrestricted use means that researchers and data managers need to be trained and persuaded to publish their data. Strategies have to be developed to evaluate the quality of data sets, models or code, and to measure their impact. Once the data is online, different levels of access have to be managed and the data's security has to be maintained.

In the networks in which all these activities take place, institutions perform varying and multiple roles and functions, often in collaboration with other institutions, and this open data ecosystem is still evolving. For many institutions, open access to research data is a new development that they are just coming to grips with, and they are not well integrated into the open data movement. Moreover, it is a new ambition or requirement to add to their many existing priorities. As various reports, roadmaps and policy documents have pointed out, enabling open access to research data and successfully exploiting the various approaches, thus requires changes in research cultures, infrastructures and funding models (see, for example, The Royal Society 2012 and Higher Level Expert Group 2010). For many institutions, the expectations expressed in such policy guidelines and roadmaps mean that they are obliged to take on new responsibilities as well as exploring and developing new practices.

Policy reports such as the influential Royal Society's report on open data (2010) generally expect universities, research institutes, libraries and funding bodies to take a leading role in enabling these changes in culture and infrastructure creation. For instance, The Royal Society recommends that:

> Universities and research institutes should play a major role in support-
> ing an open data culture [...] Learned societies, academies, and profes-
> sional bodies should promote the priorities of open science amongst
> their members and seek to secure financially sustainable open access to

journal articles. They should explore how enhanced data management could benefit their constituency and how habits might need to change to achieve this (p. 10).

The Royal Society sees a role for universities and research institutes in: adopting open data as a default position; evaluating researchers on their data sharing; developing strategies and policies for taking care of their own knowledge resources; and offering services to support researchers with their data management. They are also expected to provide funds to encourage culture change and to ensure sustainability of any resources and infrastructure that are developed.

Libraries have also become increasingly important in research data management. From a review of the literature, Cox and Pinfield (2013) find that libraries may provide services regarding research data management such as: offering advice on funding sources; promoting open access; data analysis advice; guidance on research data citation and copyright issues; and technical advice on data formats and metadata. For many libraries, this is uncharted territory, so providing these services requires the adoption of new processes and skills (The Royal Society 2011, p. 63). Furthermore, libraries are often seen as the executors of data strategies and policies, as many of the responsibilities assigned to a research institution or university are realised through their library or data repository.

In practice, it is often unclear which stakeholder is responsible for what. Many issues cross stakeholder groups, due to the complexity of the data journey (from collection through to making the data open access for reuse). For example, training and skills development are seen to be the responsibility of various stakeholders: governments should adapt new policies for data management skills to be taught at university and secondary school level; funders should educate their grant-holders about data management and institutions, with the help of libraries; and IT departments should provide training for their researchers and other staff on data management (Noorman *et al.* 2014). Researchers should also serve as mentors to early investigators and students who are interested in pursuing data sciences (National Science Board 2005). Such diffuse and, sometimes, conflicting roles and responsibilities can complicate the process of making research data freely accessible. Moreover, each research project may allocate responsibility in different ways.

Nevertheless, funders and policymakers are placing an increasing emphasis on the coordinating role of institutions, particularly regarding what they perceive as a revolutionary shift in science towards more large-scale collaborative and global research projects, which are facilitated by extensive data infrastructures (Noorman *et al.* forthcoming).

Challenges

Research for the RECODE project indicated that some institutions have already made considerable progress in sharing data and providing open access to data. Several large international consortia have, for example, created institutions to manage huge amounts of research data, such as the CERN data centre and the European Bioinformatics Institute. Other institutions have embraced the idea of open access and begun to take steps towards transforming their data-sharing practices. Yet, developments are still at an early stage and making research data publicly available has proven to be a considerable challenge in most disciplines, with approaches that work in one field not necessarily working in another (Tsoukala *et al.* 2015).

The values and norms of research practices within different disciplines shape the ways that researchers produce their data and make them openly accessible (Leonelli 2014). As discussed in more detail in Chapter Six, research practices encompass discipline-specific knowledge bases, technical tools, research teams, laboratories and culture as well as subject ethics and moral positions. These practices vary widely across disciplines and sub-disciplines, as science is made up of multiple epistemic communities producing very different products (Knorr Cetina 1999), and each community has different ideas about the significance of open data. For instance, whereas archaeology has relatively limited experience of sharing data and open data, bioengineering has a longer tradition of openly sharing models and methods, but not raw data. Established ethical and moral frameworks constrain the volume of data that is openly shared in health and clinical studies. The need to share expensive and large-scale equipment, such as telescopes and particle accelerators, has encouraged the particle physics community to establish effective data-sharing practices within large-scale global collaborations. Open data are, thus, embedded and enacted differently in different research practices, which are discussed in more detail in Chapter Six. The awareness, knowledge and infrastructure required to make data openly available is not, however, equally distributed across the scientific landscape.

This section focuses on the challenges involved in navigating between the competing interests of heterogeneous stakeholders, entrenched institutional cultures and wide-ranging and sometimes contradictory ideas about open data. Institutions often have different audiences, multiple funders and diverse ambitions. This can lead to conflicting requirements and expectations, for instance, about the quality or preservation of data, or the allocation of responsibility. It can also result in additional demands being made on an institution's often already-stretched capacity. The organisational culture within an institution can also be a barrier to making data open. Institutions generally have multiple functions and ambitions that have shaped the roles, skills and practices within them, and these do not always coincide with what is needed to make data openly accessible. Finally, it is difficult – if not impossible – to define what constitutes data, because data can take different forms in different disciplines.

The following section explores challenges in three different areas – financial support, data curation and quality control, and training and education – and discusses how various institutions have taken steps to address them.

Financial support

One of the key challenges institutions face is securing funds for open research data and, as noted in Chapter Three, the level of financial and other resources impacts on the development of open data. Efficiency gains through the reuse of data and the avoidance of duplication of data collecting and producing efforts are an important driver for open access to research data (OECD 2007; High Level Expert Group 2010). However, despite the potential cost savings that open access to research may bring in the future, preparing, archiving and making data freely accessible can be expensive, depending on the characteristics of the data to be stored, searched and used. Costs can be particularly high in data-intensive research fields, where there are extremely large data sets and high-tech computing equipment is required to process and interpret the data. In the RECODE particle physics case study, for instance, making and keeping data available to a wider public is an expensive process, because of the sheer amount of effort and resources needed to produce and store the data. Moreover, users need extensive computational resources and specialised knowledge in order to access and interpret the data. Yet, the costs of making data freely available and easily accessible may also press heavily on the available research budgets for smaller individual projects (Sveinsdottir 2013).

To make data openly accessible, funds must be secured for various phases in the data lifecycle, including the preparation, processing, sharing and archiving of data (Parse.Insight 2010). Researchers need to spend time formatting data, adding metadata and making them accessible. Archives, data centres and repositories incur significant expenses for this acquisition, processing and access, such as personnel wages, training costs for researchers and (data) librarians and outreach programmes (Beagrie *et al.* 2010). They also have to invest in the development and use of the technical infrastructure required, including the hardware needed to store the data and the software tools to use them. Moreover, increasing volumes of open research data may change existing practices and introduce new ones that will require funding and resourcing. For instance, monitoring access to data or maintaining the integrity of data may generate new costs. It may also require establishing an ethics board or developing and implementing additional administrative and editorial procedures. These requirements show that resources are needed by institutions to translate the vision of open data advocates, as described in Chapter Three, into a working institutionally supported ecosystem.

As the open access movement grows, governments, funding agencies, universities and libraries have allocated increasing funding and have developed policies to stimulate open data resources and sharing (Mossink *et al.* 2013; DCC 2012). Funding agencies have used two main funding strategies. First, through funding researchers and their projects, they have contributed to the development of open data infrastructures. Subject data repositories developed as part of research projects tend to be financed in this way. However, there are limited and uneven numbers of subject-specific data centres and repositories (Cox and Pinfield 2013) and institutions are often expected to maintain outputs in the long term for research that falls outside the remit of these centres and repositories. Second, funding bodies have attempted to stimulate open access by directly investing in developing and maintaining data centres and repositories, which offer data services to researchers and research groups, often at no cost. Science and medical funders frequently contribute to this kind of joint initiative, for example, at the European Bioinformatics Institute.

It is not immediately clear which institution should bear the responsibility for funding the many tasks involved in open data. Institutions tend to consider researchers responsible for obtaining financing for the publication and curation of their data. As data producers, scientists are viewed as the starting point of the data journey, so they are deemed responsible for ensuring data quality, ethical data collection and clear communication of data, e.g. the writing of metadata and context. Nevertheless, the top-down push for open access has also created responsibilities in terms of funding the activities required. Research communities look towards national and transnational funding bodies as well as research institutes to provide resources that will enable them to implement the various mandates and policies. Funding bodies in particular are expected to make funds available to support open data. They are seen to be responsible for providing – or at least investing in – infrastructure, in the form of data repositories, which will store data from research they have funded (OKF 2013).

The heterogeneity of data sets and associated requirements in the wide variety of disciplines adds to the challenge of financing the various phases of open research data. Institutions are now obliged to find ways to provide various services for different kinds of research, often on a limited budget. For instance, data from psychology experiments require different kinds of data management than field notes from archaeological excavations. Universities, national data centres and libraries have all stepped in to provide infrastructure and financial resources to preserve data sets that fall outside the remits of existing repositories and data centres but, as the number of such data sets grows, this may not be a sustainable option for all of them. The curation of open data continues to require resources, i.e. staff or volunteers with suitable skills and expertise are needed to keep the data up-to-date and accessible. They will have to make decisions about issues, such as what data to keep and how to transfer them to new technologies or formats. To stimulate their use, an effort has to be made to bring the data to the attention of relevant audiences. Universities and libraries will need 'larger budgets and highly skilled staff if the roles that are suggested are to be fulfilled by institution, such as universities' (The Royal Society 2012, p. 67). This raises the question of what should be funded. Some disciplines produce petabytes of data, which cannot all be stored, while some data sets might not appear interesting or useful enough to keep – although it is difficult to predict what will become valuable data in the future. As the volume and number of data sets grows, institutions will have to start making decisions about what data to keep and how to store it. They will have to develop strategies for choosing what to invest in, and these decisions may be affected by public demands for outcomes and results.

Several initiatives offer potential solutions to some of these challenges. Based on its analysis of the costs of data preservation, Jisc recommends that institutions should 'take advantage of economies of scale, using multi-institutional collaboration and outsourcing as appropriate' (Beagrie no date). In an effort to achieve this, some institutions have started to collaborate in offering data services. Several universities around the world have also established data repositories, sometimes as collaborative initiatives between multiple universities. One example of this is the collaboration between the Dutch Data Archiving and Networked Services institute

(DANS) and several archives and libraries in a federated data infrastructure, which is based on a front-office/back-office model (*Dillo et al.* 2013). This federated system comprises a network of local data stewards who are close to scientific practices, combined with centralised data services. DANS, jointly funded by the Royal Netherlands Academy for the Arts and Sciences (KNAW) and the Netherlands Organisation for Scientific Research (NWO), provides free storage and preservation for data sets in the humanities, social sciences and other disciplines (DANS, no date). DANS also runs the Dutch Dataverse Network, 'an open source application to publish, share, reference, extract and analyse research data,' which was first developed at Harvard University (The Dataverse Network project, no date). A number of databases or disciplinary repositories have arisen following collaboration between multiple universities, research institutes, funding agencies and governments, and some of these consortia have successfully obtained funding for data preservation for longer periods of time. For instance, the International Nucleotide Sequence Database Collaboration has developed and maintained three databases – DNA Data Bank of Japan, European Nucleotide Archive, and GenBank – for over 18 years. These databases receive funding from member institutions, project grants, funding bodies and governments.

Some institutions have begun exploring new ways of recovering the costs of open data. For example, several data centres have started charging for access to their larger data sets. The Dryad Digital Repository, which provides open access to research data underlying scientific publications, has developed a business and sustainability plan based on a combination of membership fees, data publishing charges (DPCs) and project grants (Dryad 2013). A diverse range of stakeholders, including journals, research institutions, publishers and scientific societies, can become a member and pay a fee, in exchange for a say in the governance of the organisation and discounts on submission fees. There have also been initiatives to tackle the challenge of long-term curation. University College London (UCL) has attempted to address part of this challenge by offering three different services: data storage services for the run-time of the project; data preservation services; and access services. By offering storage for the run-time of the experiment, UCL aims to encourage researchers to think about what will happen to the data after the project ends. Several funding bodies also now require applicants to specify how their data will be preserved longer-term as part of their applications for funding.

Although financial support for open data remains a challenge, this section has shown that more funding is becoming available from the traditional channels of research funding – for both researchers and data infrastructure. At the same time, various institutions have also started experimenting with alternative ways to cover their open research data costs. Institutions are building new alliances and exploring new organisational structures that will address the challenge of funding open data.

Data curation and quality control

An important aspect of curating open data is ensuring and maintaining their quality, with a view to enabling their reuse. To ensure that open research data is of value to research communities, researchers need to have some level of confidence in the trustworthiness and integrity of data sets, and in data repositories. Open data sets and metadata that contain significant inconsistencies, inaccuracies, flaws or that are incomplete are unsatisfactory and hard to work with.

In many disciplines, some formal and informal mechanisms are already in place to assess the quality of data at various stages of the data lifecycle. Research communities may perform several review processes, manually and automatically validating data. Data may be checked as part of the automated processes that control scientific instruments, for instance, through completeness or consistency checks, file format validation, metadata checks, storage integrity verification and tools for annotating the quality information (APARSEN 2012). Such automated procedures can quickly process data and identify and problems in real time. Nevertheless, expert knowledge may still be needed to make appropriate decisions on how to treat data which is flagged as problematic (Campbell *et al.* 2013), because automatic quality checks usually focus on just the technical quality, e.g. the completeness of the metadata or the consistency of the data. Assessing its scientific quality means evaluating data and metadata content, by considering aspects such as whether appropriate methods were used to collect the data, or if the data accurately reflect actual observations or responses. Evaluating data on that level usually requires expert knowledge and can only be achieved through peer review or appraisal by a dedicated subject specialist. Scientific practices also tend to have built-in self-correcting mechanisms, such as replicating experiments or using publicly-available sources, which encourages researchers to produce high-quality data (KNAW 2013).

Open access to high-quality research data requires additional efforts and expertise to ensure, for instance, that data are interpretable, assessable and reusable (Swan *et al.* 2008; The Royal Society 2012). A complicating factor is that ideas about what comprises a sufficient level of quality will differ, depending on who produces, manages or uses the data. Institutions providing access to public sector data for researchers, commercial organisations or citizens may have to deal with competing interests in setting their quality standards. The varying forms of data also raise questions about which, and when, data should be published – for example, should raw data be made available as early as possible, or should the data be processed first, losing some information, but making it easier for others to interpret and reuse?

One of the most important barriers that institutions face in evaluating and maintaining the quality of open data lies in the blurred distribution of responsibilities among stakeholders (Pearlman *et al.* 2013). Data quality issues entail the involvement of a variety of stakeholders in the data ecosystem, such as research funders, universities, data centres, repositories and researchers, at different stages of the data lifecycle. The role of researchers is central for data quality, as responsibility rests with them during the first stage of the data lifecycle, as part of their overall responsibility for undertaking research that is valid, accurate and ethical. However, engaging researchers in developing quality assurance practices poses a challenge in many disciplines. In particular, issues related to data management seem counter-productive to many researchers, who feel that it will require significant work to make their data accessible and reusable, but they will not be rewarded for doing this work (Kuipers and Van der Hoeven 2009). This is because, often, current institutional structures are not set up to reward researchers for their added work in terms of funding, promotion or knowledge gain. At the same time, data centres and libraries are the main actors being assigned responsibility for ensuring the quality of data, but they often lack the time or expertise to determine the level of quality. Data centres, institutional repositories and publishers serving diverse research groups have to make decisions about the extent to which they invest in ensuring the quality and integrity of data sets from various disciplines. Many institutions consulted within RECODE reported that it was too expensive to employ several data librarians or data scientists who are specialists in particular subjects and therefore capable of quality assessment. Moreover, as reviewing practices are community-specific and dependent on the form of data, it is difficult for repositories or publishers to formulate recommendations about data quality for every discipline and data type.

Various institutions have taken up the challenge of the quality of open data and have assumed a coordinating role in this evolving landscape. For example, the RECODE project found that some academic journals are contributing to quality assuring research data by developing standards,

methods and criteria for reviewing data effectively. They formulate requirements regarding data documentation and incorporate these in their
editorial policies. Furthermore, increasing numbers of journals demand
that the research data supporting articles they publish should be openly
accessible. An example is the PLOS policy, which requires such research data
to be openly available through an appropriate repository (Bloom 2013). This
policy mandates that the research data should be recorded and deposited
according to disciplinary standards, and it provides extensive references
and links to discipline-specific bodies' data documentation requirements
to support this. Several publishers and journals also compel their reviewers
to check the underlying data before they will publish submitted research
(Penev *et al.* 2011). Another example where institutions are working to
ensure the quality of open data is the increasing use of, and demand for
data management plans (DMPs). DMPs have become a commonly-used
means to encourage researchers and research groups to ensure the integrity
and quality of their data. Funders, universities and data centres are increasingly encouraging or, even mandating researchers to develop a DMP at the
beginning of their research projects. Such a plan should specify things such
as how the researchers intend to ensure the quality of their research data
(see, for example, University of Edinburgh 2014). Through such initiatives,
institutions position themselves as having leading or coordinating roles in
open data, setting standards for what is considered to be good-quality data.

The demand for high-quality open data has not only generated new
practices and activities for institutions, it has also contributed to the
development of new kinds of scientific communication. A relatively new
type of publication is data journals,[2] which publish articles that discuss
data sets that are openly available in (certified) repositories, in terms of
acquisition, methods, processing, etc. These articles describe the data
acquisition process and discuss the considerations around experimental
design (Gorgolewski *et al.* 2014), but they do not provide any analysis or
results. Nevertheless, the articles undergo peer review, as do the underlying
data. These types of publications draw attention to the significance of
research data as independent publication objects as well as considering
their quality and potential for reuse (Mayernik *et al.* 2014). They also help to
establish good practices, such as referencing data and making them available through accredited repositories. Another example is the emergence of
new mechanisms to enhance data quality, for instance through providing

2   Ubiquity Press is a well-known publisher of data journals in the humanities: http://www.
ubiquitypress.com/.

platforms where researchers can discuss data sets, or tools that can be used for altmetrics. Altmetrics is the study and use of scholarly impact measures, based on activity in online tools and environments. According to the Altmetrics manifesto, 'altmetrics expands our view of what impact looks like, but also of what's making the impact' (Roemer *et al.* 2013).

However, RECODE has also found that evaluating and maintaining the quality of data, both in terms of bits and bytes as well as scientific value, requires considerable work and significant changes in organisational and cultural practices. Peer review strategies have to be developed; data citation practices have to be actively encouraged and made part of institutional evaluation and reward systems. The initiatives described above illustrate that some institutions, often in collaboration with research communities, have developed a range of tools, practices and relationships to ensure the quality of open data. In order to accommodate the heterogeneous demands for data quality from a wide variety of stakeholders, there is a need for institutions to develop new roles and relationships. Publishers, data centres and libraries are therefore collaborating to encourage changes in existing cultures and to offer incentives to make research communities prioritise their data management and quality assurance.

Training and education

Various reports and roadmaps assign institutions a key role in encouraging researchers to develop open data practices. 'Scientists need to take action to make their data available but it is up to supporting institutions to clear barriers and facilitate this process, by offering incentives and infrastructure' (The Royal Society 2012, p. 10). Institutions are expected to encourage researchers to open up and share their data as well as using existing open data, by building support infrastructures, offering support and education.

Encouraging and enabling researchers to publish and share their data is posing a significant challenge for institutions. Many repositories that were created to encourage open access publications and data sharing remain almost empty. Borgman (2012) notes that, despite significant investments in, and promotion of data sharing, the 'dirty little secret' is that very little data sharing is actually taking place (Borgman 2012, p. 1060). She notes that relatively few studies show any consistent data release, and data sharing seems to be concentrated in a few fields. '[L]ittle research data is [sic] circulated beyond the research teams that produce them, and few requests are made for these data' (*Ibid.*). Studies indicate that researchers are reluctant to share their data because of various concerns, ranging from being scooped, to being unable to protect the privacy of their research subjects (Kuipers and Van der Hoeven, 2009). Moreover, open access to research data requires specific skills and knowledge that have to be developed and maintained. Yet, researchers are reluctant to participate in training courses, unless they are directly relevant for their research. Another study showed that researchers are unfamiliar with terms like 'digital curation' and 'digital repository', and suspicious of policies that issue various requirements and mandates. They prefer advice that conveys a sense of purpose and assistance (Freimna *et al.* 2010).

In addition, RECODE also found that institutions are also facing several barriers. Multiple conceptions of open data make it difficult for librarians and data centre professionals to help researchers across the board. Every discipline and sub-discipline requires a different kind of data expertise. Moreover, it can be difficult for librarians and data curators to make the connection between the relatively new and rapidly-evolving field of digital data management and the everyday practice of doing research. Cox and Pinfield argue that it is 'like any area of specialist activity – complex and jargon ridden,' and assert that a 'whole social world of organisations, projects, thought-leaders and key influencers, technologies, discourses, concepts and terminology has to be mastered in order to be 'taken seriously'' (2013, p. 4). Librarians may find it difficult to acquire sufficient technical knowledge of digital data management to position themselves as key players, while also maintaining domain-specific expertise and knowledge of doing research.

The established institutional culture may also represent a barrier, because open access to research data is just one of many competing priorities. Moreover, various parts of an organisation each have their own set of ambitions, so it can be a considerable challenge to raise making more research data open up the agenda, when other concerns take priority. Further progress in the area of training and skills development can also be hampered by the balance of power. Librarians may establish and administer the institutional repository with significant knowledge about scholarly communication issues but, since they do not bring any funding into the university, the library is generally perceived as a service-based unit that lacks much strategic influence. Thus, the distribution of responsibility often remains unclear. One study on research data management notes the lack of professional preparation. '[A]lmost no one within the academic community receives systematic professional training and certification in the management of research data. Still worse [...] virtually no one in academia perceives that they have a professional responsibility or mandate for research data management functions' (Halbert 2013).

In some disciplines, such as particle physics, genetics or social geography, digital data management training is already an integral part of the (post-graduate) curriculum, but it remains a relatively new area in many subject areas. There are very few disciplinary-focused data curation training programmes at universities (Creamer *et al.* 2012; Walters 2009; Lyon 2012). Universities, departments, research groups and research institutes are only just beginning to gain experience of providing appropriate courses, workshops and tools to support researchers, librarians, information specialists and other staff in their data management activities. Important developments in this respect are the increasing number of training programmes and materials that data centres, libraries and research consortia are offering for researchers as well as the establishment of professional training programmes for data curators and information specialists. The training available for data management and curation is mainly provided by dedicated national bodies, libraries, information science schools or data centres. The UK Digital Curation Centre (DCC) plays a leading role in offering training for practitioners in need of resources on data management. The DCC offers workshops in data management as well as short, intensive half-day or three-day courses for absolute beginners (Keralis 2012). They also offer information and a range of tools to help researchers prepare their data management plans. The DANS institute provides various workshops, training courses and guest lectures for researchers and students in the humanities and social sciences at various Dutch universities and research institutions (DANS, no date).

In addition to these training initiatives from dedicated projects and organisations, some promising practices are emerging within universities. For example, the University of Southampton has, through collaboration with the UK Research Data Service and involvement in projects like the Institutional Data Management Blueprint Project (IDMB), worked to improve and formalise initiatives to support their university researchers to manage their research data (Brown and White 2013). The university aims to develop an understanding of different disciplinary needs through partnership and cooperation, to implement simple, low-cost technical solutions and applications, and to focus on training and support. Another example is the UK Orbital project at the University of Lincoln's School of Engineering. The project has proposed a set of recommendations to support further development of their research data management structure (Stainthorp 2012). This project underlines the fact that researchers are heterogeneous not only in terms of discipline, but also between individuals in the same team. It is, therefore, important to gain an understanding of the culture within any given set of researchers before considering how to influence their research data management behaviour.

Libraries are also considered well suited to playing a greater role in guiding researchers' data management practices. Libraries have a long tradition of subject liaison staff, who work closely with researchers to understand their needs, so they could comprise the 'last mile' of research data infrastructures – 'the part of the network that will provide connections between the systems and the researchers, and ultimately, to new users of the data' (Gabridge 2009). Librarians could take on the role of data stewards for various stakeholders, especially researchers, by activities such as organising conferences, distributing literature, devising training courses, web tutorials and advocacy programmes tailored for specific research communities. Indeed, several physical and digital libraries, such as the Edinburgh University Library and the California Digital library, have started to develop this new intermediary role. They liaise with researchers and help them to deposit their data at the point of creation, provide advice about data standards, and create curation plans for the whole data lifecycle, in compliance with funder mandates. They also provide seminars and workshops or individual tuition for research and professional staff.

Open access to research data requires specific skills and knowledge that have to be developed and maintained. As this section shows, several institutions have taken up the challenge of educating and training researchers, librarians, information and data scientists and other professionals, building on existing and emerging digital data management practices. Libraries, data repositories, data centres and dedicated organisations, such as the DCC, have become advocates of data sharing and open access, and position themselves as valuable resource-providers for knowledge and expertise about open data.

Conclusion

Institutions such as universities, libraries, data centres, publishers, professional associations and funding bodies, are all playing an important role in making research data open. They support researchers, provide infrastructure and funding, and set best practice guidelines. Open access to research data offers many benefits, but some challenges still need to be overcome if these gains are to be realised.

One of these is the fact that, although open access may produce significant cost savings in the long term, it generates considerable costs in the short term. Open access requires significant and continuous effort to make sure that data can be found, interpreted, evaluated and used. Another challenge is the relatively low level of data management skills and awareness about the opportunities and limitations of open research data that exists in institutions and many research communities. Cutting across these challenges are issues concerning the heterogeneity of the stakeholders, the multiple conceptions of open data and entrenched institutional cultures. Importantly, none of these challenges are specific to open access to research data, and need to be addressed by stakeholders within big data or open government data as well.

Developments in the data ecosystem that address these challenges are still in the early stages, but they indicate major shifts in roles, responsibilities and relationships within the research landscape. Whereas researchers in many disciplines used to be responsible for their own data, even after their projects had finished, this responsibility is now partly delegated to data centres and repositories. Institutions such as universities, funders, publishers and libraries have taken on coordinating roles in training, education and setting standards for data quality. They have begun to offer data services, establish infrastructures and issue policies. In terms of financial resources, knowledge and expertise, several institutions have engaged in collaborative efforts to develop data repositories, data management services, training programmes, etc. Libraries are working with data centres and other libraries to offer long-term preservation of, and access to, research data, as well as skills development programmes. Universities, research institutes, and funding bodies are participating in international collaborations. Indeed, through building alliances and (trans)national collaboration, some institutions have already become important actors in the data ecosystem, giving shape to a diversity of access arrangements and governance structures. In order to achieve a knowledge society, these stakeholders must continue this work, and stakeholders within other open data ecosystems need to be encouraged to take such leadership and coordination roles. This is happening in many contexts, but it needs to be significantly expanded, especially in relation to the citizen participation aspirations of many open data advocates.

Within the scholarly landscape, institutions are playing an increasingly important role in opening up knowledge to a broader public. Nevertheless, as this chapter has shown, opening up data in any context raises significant challenges, and making data available will not necessarily result in ease of use or accessibility across the board. In order for institutions within all of the data ecosystems to contribute to a data-capable and well-informed society, they will have to invest more into a support structure that will enable a diverse range of people to find, access, interpret and use data.

6. Mobilising data

Scientific disciplines, scientific practice and making research data open

Introduction

This chapter addresses some of the details in making data open from the point of view of those who produce data and knowledge – researchers. Although open data advocates have produced some guidelines for making data open, they do not specifically address how researchers should work with specific types of data. Furthermore, open data policy documents such as the EC's Recommendation on providing open access to scientific information (2012) and the OECD Principles and Guidelines (2007) only attend to data in a very general way and do not address the way in which data is produced, managed and interpreted through particular types of research or information practices.

The chapter uses information from the five RECODE disciplinary case studies – archaeology, bioengineering, environmental research, health and clinical research, and particle physics – to gain an understanding of specific types of research practice. This examination of research practice considers the relationship between specific sets of research practice and how to make data open.

Areas within which data is produced are science, social sciences and humanities. In this context, the move towards data openness is tied to wider sweeping changes towards open science or science 2.0, which include attempts to open up the scientific process for review and comment in ways including open methodology, open source, open peer review and open access to publications) (see, e.g. Pontika *et al.* 2015) In general terms, policymakers and open data advocates are seeking to create changes in the ways that data is managed and shared, in order to reap the full benefits that data is perceived to offer. However, less attention is paid to the ways in which particular sectors and disciplines produce and manage data, and what this means for making data open. Scientific and academic disciplines face particular challenges in making data open because of the specific ways in which their research is conducted, their histories, research cultures and different epistemologies and methodologies as well as differing views on data. Certain disciplines also yield different types of data, much of which may not be suitable for open access due to various factors, such as size, complexity and ethical issues, which will be explored further in this chapter.

This chapter first considers how the drive towards open access to publicly-funded research data is being driven by the idea that science and scientific results are a public good. Second, the chapter discusses case study findings from literature review, interviews and workshops with researchers and other stakeholders from five different disciplines – archaeology, bioengineering, environmental research, health and clinical research, and particle physics, to examine how scientists are negotiating the drive towards open data within their discipline-specific contexts, and what their key challenges and opportunities are. This offers a particular opportunity to understand the extent to which these stakeholders have been, or can be, mobilised within the open data movement (discussed in Chapter Four) to further progress towards a knowledge society.

The construction and production of data is shaped by the design of any research project and in the practice of research. This chapter discusses the way in which researchers – those actively involved in the production of data – interpret what open data means for the practice of research. The overarching assessment is that the research process needs to adopt a stronger focus on yielding reusable data sets that can be made openly available. The chapter will also highlight the increasing, emergent complexity of contemporary scientific practice with respect to interdisciplinary research, sophisticated technology (e.g. simulations), international collaborations and data size, considering how all of these elements may complicate the process of research and, consequently, the production, analysis and openness of research data.

The policy drive towards open research data

Examining much of the high-level science policy and grey literature that reflects on the changing ways in which science is conducted (open science or science 2.0), it is apparent that the link between science practice, research data and the benefits of openness are often referred to as being self-evident. Open data is seen to offer 'reduced duplication of data collection costs and increased transparency of the scientific record; increased research impact and reduced time-lag in realising those impacts' (Fry *et al*, 2008, p. iv), and it also 'speeds up scientific progress and helps combat scientific fraud' (The European Commission 2012, p. 3). Efforts to provide open access to publicly-funded research data are often supported by references to public funding and interest, the concept of social responsibility and responsible research and innovation (RRI) (European Commission 2012, 2015). It is presumed that integrating and linking data will facilitate the creation of new knowledge, while data reuse will also ensure validation and quality control of data and scientific research more broadly (OECD 2007). Data users are seen to comprise researchers, policymakers, businesses and citizens, and there is a belief that each of these will advance within their own domains through the democratisation of knowledge, which will lead to a more informed public that is better able to participate in social debates and the development of society (UNESCO 2012).

Open access to research data is also seen as a way to bring knowledge closer to the public and be useful to various actors in society (e.g. industry and government) for further innovation and, consequently, social and economic benefit, in line with the key aims of the Mode 2 paradigm of knowledge production as outlined by Gibbons *et al.* (1994). In policy documents, science is often referred to as a single field (European Commission 2014; The Royal Society 2012), which, to some extent, risks obscuring the differences that exist within it, with regard to scientific disciplines, research practices, methodologies and types of data. However, the case study research of five scientific disciplines reveals that, in order to implement open access to research data, different disciplines will need to consider the role of data in their research practices and consider how it can be made reusable and accessible within and outside the field of science.

Disciplinary negotiations around implementing open access to research data

Research interviews with 29 scientists within the five disciplines of archaeology, bioengineering, environmental research, health and clinical research and particle physics[1] revealed the often-complex negotiations of integrating open access to research data with already established research practices. The interviews showed that each discipline is currently in a different stage of data openness. Although the scientists are accustomed to sharing data with selected users such as within research groups, project consortia and colleagues, it is less common for them to contribute to open data, which

1   This research was done as part of the European Commission-funded 'RECODE' research project and was published in the report 'D1.1 Stakeholder Values and Ecosystems': http://recodeproject.eu/wp-content/uploads/2013/10/RECODE_D1-Stakeholder-values-and-ecosystems_Sept2013.pdf.

is available to all potential users online. The notion of openness flags up many complex questions like, for instance, how it can be integrated with established research practices, the data that they yield, ethical considerations, the size of data sets and the resources needed to prepare the data and keep it openly accessible.

Archaeology was described by respondents as a relatively 'closed' discipline, as standard archaeological research practices made it unusual to share or release data for open access. Archaeology was described as an individual pursuit, and monographs were highly rated in terms of career progression. Because of the nature of their subjects (human physiological processes and the natural and built environment), bioengineering and environmental research were described as open, with high levels of data sharing and open data, the latter more applicable to environment sciences, since bioengineering tends to share models rather than data. With regard to health and clinical research, respondents described how data sharing within large project consortia was more common than open data, due to ethical issues and IPR. A similar story emerged from respondents within the particle physics case study, where data sharing is common within international project consortia, but openness is considered impossible, especially due to the sheer size of many particle physics data sets.

Some issues were the same across disciplines, such as lack of funding for, and recognition of data work. Raw data could only be shared in a few cases, and a significant amount of work would be required to make the data usable, by writing metadata, cleaning, coding and anonymising data and, in some instances, providing accompanying models and software to make the data understandable and assessable (The Royal Society 2012). Without this work, users are ill-equipped to use open data. The publishing of a good data set is not yet widely recognised by institutions as a worthwhile activity in terms of career progression, where publications in peer-reviewed journals still weigh most heavily. Concerns were raised by scientists within archaeology, bioengineering, environment sciences and health and clinical research about making sensitive information, such as human and location data open, as this could have serious consequences for human subjects and place certain localities, such as burial sites and sacred places at risk.

The following sections describe the disciplinary contexts and discipline-specific negotiations currently taking place within these five academic disciplines, as they start to implement open access to their data.

Archaeology

The archaeology respondents all agreed that open research data had benefits and value for archaeology as a discipline, which holds legacy data sets[2] and depends on cumulative data collection from excavation sites, which sometimes span decades of notes, data, artefacts, photographs and drawings from any one site. The scientists agreed that there would be great value in making data accessible for archaeologists, but expressed concern that this would take a lot of time and effort, as much of the legacy data is not in digital format. Another key barrier was grounded in the often-individualistic approaches to the practice of archaeology, in terms of documenting, coding, archiving and analysing excavation data:

> I think in the past, people did it their own way and everyone did it differently and you didn't ever expect to show it to anyone. I think in many cases it was messier and not as well documented. You didn't have to expose it. [...] Archaeology is also quite different in the way that there are very few examples of collaborations where people have integrated data sets. There is not a tradition of collaboration. There are mostly single authored publications (senior researcher A, archaeology).

In the interviews, archaeology was described as a discipline where individual approaches are undertaken, and publications in the form of monographs are highly valued. A scientist may work on one excavation site for a number of years, accumulating data in phases. This has yielded large data sets that may, in some instances, be unusable for outside users, due to the often idiosyncratic and individualistic ways in which data has been organised, coded and analysed:

> the interesting issue was that one data set would have molluscs in it and another data set from a nearby site would have none and the question would be, did this site not have any molluscs in it, or was it that the molluscs were being analysed by another researcher and were not present in the data set? So, these issues can be very challenging when you get into data integration (senior researcher B, archaeology).

---

2   David Plaza (no date) defines legacy data sets in archaeology as 'old, not in use, in a state of disrepair and obsolete' and describes the process of digitisation as a way to transfer a legacy data set into 'living documents.'

The archaeologists also described their discipline as being slow moving, in the sense that scientists rely on cumulative data for their publications, which can take a few years to gather before publishing. The fear of being scooped as a consequence of opening up data too early could, therefore, be a difficult barrier within archaeology. Furthermore, the fear of being criticised was also mentioned as a potential barrier, but the opportunity for correction and academic scrutiny was seen as an opportunity that would hopefully outweigh the former and would drive the faster implementation of open access policies and traditions within archaeology.

Bioengineering

The bioengineering respondents all recognised the value of openness for advancing their field, publishing good-quality, reviewed data, minimising duplication of effort and producing knowledge that could be built on further. However, in the bioengineering interviews, two key stories emerged. Firstly, that bioengineering is an open discipline, in the sense that it has long-standing experience of sharing models, code and – to some extent – data, but not experimental or raw data. Secondly, that these initiatives were linked to specific institutions or research groups, with researchers outside those groups stating that there were, however, still considerable disciplinary and institutional barriers to opening up access to models and data. Competition within the discipline was named as a key obstacle, as was the lack of infrastructure, such as repositories, in which to store and make data available, along with legal and ethical barriers against making human and patient data openly available. A lack of metadata standards was also named as a barrier as well as the lack of recognition of the work entailed in preparing both models and data for publication:

> I think it is principally because of the lack of standards available for describing the data. At least in the case of models we have put a fair bit of thought into the provenance of models. [...] what it does require is an enormous investment of effort to translate models to enable them to be available publicly and there is no recognition at all for that work. That requires money and time and it is impossible to get funding for that sort of work (senior researcher, bioengineering).

Those researchers who worked with open models and data described bioengineering as an inherently open discipline due to its broad subject focus, which is the human body and function and processes of cells, tissues and organs. The complexity of building models to simulate the processes made it important that data be shared, since cumulative and integrative practices were necessary to advance knowledge and understanding of the human body and disease and illness. Sharing models, data and code should limit duplication; however, the tradition of sharing data and the lack of infrastructure and modes of peer review were all mentioned as barriers that would need to be tackled in order to successfully use open access to its fullest extent. As in archaeology, the researchers in bioengineering referred to the work involved in preparing data for open access but, more importantly, the work involved in using open access to data, which would include making sure that it was checked for errors and that the quality of the data and the metadata had undergone a thorough examination.

Environmental research

Environmental research addresses complex grand challenges and, as such, uses a multidisciplinary approach whereby researchers gather and use diverse data derived from different scientific fields and sub-fields, such as biology, forestry, agricultural research, weather research, and oceanography. Access to data, data integration and reuse are key values that underpin environmental research and its development. There is general agreement within environmental research about the benefits of open data, and the key driver of this is the overarching global challenge of environmental change and the fundamental need to understand and respond to this. The environmental scientists interviewed also considered public access to data, whether from firms or citizens, as important for helping with this endeavour. The key barriers to advancing open access to research data in the environmental research are mostly derived from the diversity of data sources and types:

> We are broadly in favour of open data but we ourselves have limitations because a lot of the data we have is not our own and is data that comes from the member states and they give us access to data. Sometimes we have to buy it, sometimes they give it to us on condition that we use it for particular pieces of work, and that limits our ability to provide it openly because intellectual property rights are a factor and it's their data not our data (director of research, environmental research).

Much of the data that environmental scientists use is obtained from the public sector and, as many of the research challenges stretch across national borders, obstacles often appear in the form of different use licences, regulations, ownership and use clauses. These may, at times, be complex, time-consuming and can limit researchers in their work. Furthermore, any one study may require satellite, forestry, flood and soil data, all of which may come from different sources and in different formats. Legal and ethical issues regarding environmental data can also form barriers to open access, and the interviewees were sceptical that all environmental data could ever be made available through open access, maintaining that some data needed access controls to protect specific locations:

> Even though (we) strive to release as much work as possible under the open data approach, for some types of data – because of external legal concerns that pertain to the data themselves, not what we do – it is impossible. We do therefore have to avoid releasing some types of data and we have, for example, units within our institute here who work on security issues. The issues of maritime protection and also navigation and releasing these types of data could lead to the wrong people getting to know some sensitive information and so we are banned from doing that (senior researcher, environmental research).

Legal and ethical issues were manifested in different ways and were mentioned in all of the case studies except particle physics. The scientists agreed that these can be a difficult obstacle to overcome, one which would require concerted consideration by disciplinary as well as legal and ethical experts.

Health and clinical research

Much like environmental research and bioengineering, health and clinical research deals with complex challenges, such as genetic medical conditions and epidemics that require multidisciplinary approaches, with each discipline contributing their specific research practices, traditions, and different view of health, disease and patients. As health and clinical research benefits from being able to link patient data from many sources, researchers from this field were positive about increasing open access to research data. However, considerable legal and privacy issues arise in relation to opening up access to genome, human and patient data:

> The concern is that combining a number of data, which are very extensive when it comes to genetic traits combining it with another database, can lead to the identification of an individual. That is somewhat of concern. I

think the NSI in the USA will be able to do that study. Bio check and they will track you down in Saudi Arabia. So, there are actually political issues. You will have to avoid anything that could identify anybody (research project coordinator, health and clinical research).

To complicate matters further, a number of different stakeholders are involved in various projects, for instance, pharmaceutical companies, patient organisations, ICT staff, journals and research institutions, each of which conduct data work differently. These consortia have strict legal agreements to protect the IPR and commercial interests of industry partners, which may either completely hinder data sharing, or limit it and request extended embargo periods. The pharmaceutical industry might be reluctant to share any commercially-sensitive data, whilst patient organisations would be unwilling to open up data because of privacy concerns.

The health researchers interviewed supported the idea of open access to research data and saw the benefits as being a reduction of duplication, faster progress on health and clinical research, and a reduced need for data collection from patient groups and the public, the former of which they felt were overly burdened with research requests.

Particle physics

Much research data within particle physics is generated by particle physics detectors that track and measure particles, in some instances over a number of years. These detectors produce large quantities of data, measured in terabytes, which are stored, processed and analysed using a grid computing approach that involves hundreds or thousands of interconnected machines around the world. Although most of the interviewees were positive about open data and understood its value for physics, they expressed doubts about whether 'big science' data, such as that generated by the large hadron collider at CERN, was suitable for open access, due to a lack of interest from people from outside physics. Scientists doubted that individuals would have access to the processing power required to download, store and analyse their enormous volumes of data. Specific software and hardware would also be needed in many instances for any significant data work to be carried out as well as a knowledge of physics and experiments, undertaken in order to fully understand the meaning of the data:

If you were to try to make the raw data available to outsiders you would have to make available the raw data, the reconstruction programs, the simulation and its database, the programs that handle the simulation and you would need to ensure there was access to the physics generators which are usually written by the theorists and not the experimenters who wrote the experimental simulation and it just gets too complicated (senior researcher, particle physics).

In addition to these complications, significant funding would be needed to make big physics data open, and the physicists interviewed stated that they would rather see such funds spent on research, rather than on making data open for the very few people who could potentially use it. The case of particle physics thus raises an important question regarding the relevance of data for open access and the assumed economic benefit of preparing and storing data for the long term, which may, in fact, only be useful to a very small group of scientists.

Examining the barriers inherent in these five disciplines demonstrates how current data work and research practices, if left unchanged, may pose a delay in realising the move towards open access to research data and, consequently, a knowledge society. It illustrates the diversity between different subject areas – small, personal data sets in archaeology through to massive data sets emerging from particle physics. It also shows how data sets from human research subjects have specific ethical issues, and simulation data from bioengineering requires the use of specific hardware, software and some knowledge about modelling in order to be properly understood.

Furthermore, research practice takes place within different constellations, from a single researcher to large consortium projects with partners from academia, industry and government. Thus, views on data, its potential and ownership may vary greatly, thus further complicating the process of making research data open. The next section will examine in more depth the potential changes that disciplines will need to implement in order to integrate open access to research data into their research practices, as seen through the eyes of practicing scientists.

Current research practices and their alignment with open access

Examining research practices within five different disciplines reveals the heterogeneity and multiplicity of approaches, traditions, histories, and research cultures within science. It became evident that for open access to data to become a part of research practices, there need to be negotiations and flexibility in approach so that so that openness gains legitimisation among researchers and mobilises them. Open access to research data will need to be embedded in current research practices, some of which may need to change to accommodate new ways of doing data work, e.g. collection, coding, analysing, archiving, etc. This section will focus on current research practices and how these may be aligned to mobilise further towards the knowledge society. The section brings to the fore three issues that emerged from all the case studies, i.e. the need to plan for data focused research so that knowledge may be shared, rewarding data work and taking into consideration data specificity and size.

Data-centred research

When discussing open access to data, the scientists interviewed referred to their current and past research activity to describe the complexities involved in making the data they had already gathered, or were in the process of gathering, available for open access. Scientists in archaeology, bioengineering and physics explained that preparing this data for open access would take a lot of work, most of which would be unfunded and would not yield demonstrable rewards in terms of career progression or prestige. They indicated that, in light of the move towards open access to research data, research practices would need to become more data focused, with data collection and openness factored in at the very start of the research cycle – at the proposal stage – to ensure that each project included the aim of creating robust data sets that would be meaningful and useful, and would outlive the primary purpose for which they were collected. The archaeology scientists welcomed the introduction of data management plans by research funders in this respect, along with the opportunity to factor data work in when applying for grant funding. However, a research director within bioengineering wished to see a stronger policy drive from research funders, so that open access to data would gain a stronger foothold within research practices. Furthermore, the current funding model and attempts to share data were felt to be a barrier because data should be shared near the end of each project, before the point when contractual obligations between researchers and research funders are coming to an end. Consequently, any demands after a project ends are likely to be unmet, as the funds have been used and contracts are no longer in place:

> Either we are serious about this policy and I am not saying this is neces-
> sarily a good idea but, as a practical example, if I am a funding agency

> and I give you £1 million for a 3 year research project and I do at the
> end a systematic review and I find that this much data is worth sharing
> with the community for the next 10 years, I give you £50,000 every year
> to sustain the data sharing to the community that is a credible policy
> (research director, bioengineering).

This would mean a shift to focus on data throughout the entire research
process, from proposal writing to releasing the data for open access. It
would feed into decision making and planning of data collection, storage,
analysis, metadata writing as well as software and hardware necessary,
considering – if applicable – how these would affect plans for openness. In
terms of ethics, consent forms and other ethical considerations, would need
to change, to account for openness of data. The researchers also mentioned
that the prospect of releasing data for open access could drive faster dissemination times, since scientists would be keen to ensure that their data
and findings would be published before their data was available through
open access. Furthermore, better data standards and research practices
were mentioned as a good outcome from openness, because researchers
would become more aware that their data could be accessed by peers as
well as broader society.

This change in research practices would also need to be integrated into
education and training for early career researchers, to instil good data
practices in preparation for openness:

> I think it would be just a slight change of culture in the sense that when
> the students are developing the model whatever they do is well annotated.
> It is not really extra work but it is just getting into the routine of doing it
> in a consistent manner, thinking that this programme could actually be
> read by lots of people including someone who does not exactly master
> the programme or English. You need to think a little bit more about how
> you provide commentary and comments to your programme, for example
> (senior researcher, bioengineering).

Scientists within archaeology, bioengineering, health and clinical research
and particle physics acknowledged that there was a tendency to perceive
research data as private, in the sense that only the researcher or researchers in any one study would have access to it, so the data sets and ways of
organising, coding, describing and analysing them would only need to make
sense to those involved. This became especially clear within archaeology,
as discussed above. However, different manifestations of this emerged from

all five disciplines studied, because data and data sets are context-specific, with data collection taking place within different research designs, for various purposes, by different data collection methods and to respond to different research questions. Consequently, to make the data sufficiently comprehensible for an outsider to use it, scientists would need to start working with their data in different ways, so that it could be used by external scientists who had not participated in the original research. Some scientists admitted that there was a need for annotation and metadata standards and a mutual defining of parameters, so that the benefits of open access to research data could be fully realised:

> people can do limited work with a data set that is not well documented. I do worry that people will just think, 'Oh I need to archive my data and then it's done', but it goes beyond archiving. The key question here is, 'is the data set going to be reusable 40 years down the line, when you are not around anymore?' Just because it is archived, does not mean it is reusable (senior researcher, archaeology).

The impacts of these changes in practices would mean that each step of the research cycle would need to include an awareness of how the resulting data could best be utilised by external scientists. Initial research design, methods, methodology, data collection, research ethics and consent, data annotation, coding, writing of metadata and archiving would need to be re-thought. This would require additional funds and working hours for each project, a fact which scientists felt was scarcely understood by funders. Furthermore, lack of time and funding was also considered a barrier to working on data sets derived from earlier studies, which could benefit researchers but which are not suitable for open access in their current form. Some data sets will require substantial work and, in some instances, first-hand experience of the research to achieve this, which would be difficult if researchers have become unavailable, e.g. through changing jobs.

Data work and recognition

The 'data work' required to release meaningful and useful data for open access, such as coding, metadata writing, formatting and organising, was referred to as a time-consuming activity, which was not adequately funded. The researchers were working within, or had past experience of working in systems within which career progression was, in part, determined by their publications record, whereas data work was not as highly regarded as peer-reviewed publications. The researchers felt that, in order to drive mobilisation towards open access, the recognition system would need to expand to take into account data work and published data sets. The researchers could not see much benefit of releasing data for open access if the system remained largely unchanged, believing that work would continue to be diverted into activities that were valued and better rewarded:

> because they (academics) need the publications to get jobs and they need the recognition, and the data set gets no recognition. It's the bottom of the barrel in terms of what might get you a job. It's like the refuse after you have consumed everything and it is too bad because those data sets can become the foundation of another research project and frequently people need that data that someone else has used (senior researcher, archaeology).

Furthermore, the scientists raised the question of 'added value', wondering whether time and funds spent on such data work would really benefit those who sought to access open research data. As much as research data is complex and may need specialist software, hardware and equipment, they were concerned that it would not be usable by scientists outside their respective field. Thus, it was likely that other scientists and citizens would not be able to use the data even if it was made available through open access. This is the question whether all data should be made open, irrespective of its added value:

> You might end up wasting millions of pounds and then only 10 people are interested, that is a waste of money and work. A small number of interesting events could be interesting for someone. I heard that 13,000 events were put forward for schools and outreach. Apparently in CERN the general public can come and look at the display and play with the data at the centre. This is interesting for the public but, to analyse an enormous amount of data, you would need resources for this (researcher, particle physics).

The need for, and recognition of, data work within contemporary contexts of research and knowledge production was a consistent theme across all five disciplines.

Contemporary research and data complexity

Many of the interviewees mentioned the current availability of research data, its many formats and the speed by which it can be produced and analysed as factors in a complicated challenge to the mobilisation towards open access. Types of data and the ways in which it is derived (for instance, computer simulation in bioengineering or handwritten notes at an archaeological excavation) also vary considerably in size, complexity and epistemological foundation.

So that an external researcher can interpret raw data which has not been processed in any way, s/he will at least require a description of the methodology used and the context within which it was collected. For derived data (i.e. data which has been processed in some way), the metadata must in addition contain a description of the formal system used to generate it:

> The important thing in my view is that data is not the only thing you need. You need to know more about the data than just the numbers that have been generated in order to interpret that in a proper way. [...] The methods and the context that have been used to collect the data are an integral part of the validity of the data (research director, health and clinical research).

Simulation data results from experiments undertaken in virtual representations of the real world, where it is not feasible to experiment with the real system, e.g. complex biological processes or climate systems. The simulation outputs also comprise derived data, but in order to make this type of data intelligible, assessable and usable, additional information would need to accompany the data, such as a description of the simulator itself, its usage, parameter values, starting conditions, and the software platforms that it ran on.

This chapter has described how data exists in its own specific context, drawing on interviews from five disciplines to illustrate this argument. Contemporary research practices are frequently carried out within complex constellations of researchers, policymakers and industry stakeholders. For data to be made meaningful and open for reuse, each research context would need clarification and explanation, which can be a complex and lengthy task and which is currently not generally a funded part of most research projects. Furthermore, in order for the open data movement to adequately motivate and mobilise these important stakeholders, individual researchers and organisations need clear information about the benefits they would gain from opening up their data, since data publications and data sets are not as highly valued or rewarded as research journal articles within the academic system. All of this clearly shows that research practices will need to change, so that mobilisation towards a knowledge society, driven by open access to research data, is successful.

Conclusion: Mobilising data

Open access to research data is one aspect of transferring knowledge. There is a current policy drive towards opening access to research data to benefit society through enabling faster innovation and economic development; however, progress has been slow.

This chapter has explored the types of disciplinary negotiations currently taking place, as scientists start integrating open access practices within already established research contexts.

Chapter Two and this chapter have both explored how and why data needs to be analysed and understood in its scientific and social context, to enable mobilisation towards a knowledge society to occur. As the interviewees from five different disciplines explained, data is poorly understood out of its context of epistemology, methodology and research practices, all of which need to be taken into account when data is made open. In most cases, data is not meaningful to secondary users in its raw form and does not stand alone, but may require extensive metadata, simulation software and specific hardware to enable secondary analysis or integration to be successfully carried out by users external to the initial production process.

In line with the framework of Mode 2 knowledge production (Gibbons *et al.* 1994), current research practices and groupings are complex and include input from societal actors such as industry, policymakers and government stakeholders. These groups may hold differing views of what data is and what it means for knowledge production, and this may complicate the process of making data open because of legal complications such as IPR and other commercial and scientific factors. Furthermore, the complicated and nuanced ethics surrounding research data that is derived from human subjects will need a specific approach to protect participants' privacy. This also applies to sensitive geographical data, around burial sites and other culturally-significant places as well as the location of important infrastructures (e.g., power plants).

The archaeology interviewee raised the issue of the – often strong – link between a researcher and their data, describing how research data is often perceived as private and closed to those external to a research project or process. This was also mentioned by researchers within the other disciplines as constituting a potential barrier against progress towards open data. As this chapter has explored, archaeology, health and clinical research and some 'big science' disciplines each have different approaches to gathering, analysing and storing data, so these practices will need to be adjusted to enable these disciplines to successfully move towards open access. To fully embrace openness, data work must be embedded within current research practices and an understanding must be reached that some data may not be suitable for opening up due to its size, complexity or IPR issues.

In order to mobilise data, research practices must be aligned to focus on data as a meaningful and shareable entity. Thus, data practices themselves must become recognised as a valued component activity of scientific research and must be integrated into the research process from start to finish. If this happens, different scientific disciplines will continue to contribute to the production of knowledge and the advancement of knowledge societies through their own research.

7. Mobilising data

Environmental data, technical and governance issues

Introduction

The argument so far has covered some of the general issues and trends in the mobilisation of open data. Chapters Three and Four show that there are a set of requirements including technological and governance ones that need to be addressed and implemented to support open data. To understand how these requirements can be realised, Chapters Five and Six explored the issues facing institutions and how making data open interacts with, and may shape, existing research practices across a range of disciplines. To address issues about data, technology and governance in making data open in detail, this chapter focuses on one context where open data is being mobilised: the environmental sector. This area of research has engaged with making data open and continues to do so; in so doing, it has revealed the issues of developing open access to data. It is also an area of research that has many characteristics of Mode 2 Knowledge production and thus it is an example of late modern science. The fact that it has gained experience about knowing how to make data open from core aspects of open data, namely the technical, governance and data aspects, and how these are related to each other, makes it a useful case to discuss. When this is combined with its Mode 2 Knowledge production characteristics, the environmental or earth sciences are an exemplar of the issues in making data open. Further, its work links closely with many of the challenges that society is facing and it therefore brings out the role of data in society to address contemporary societal grand challenges.

'Environment' is used here in its broadest terms, to include land, oceans, the atmosphere, polar regions, life, the planet's natural cycles and deep earth processes, along with the mutual influences of these constituent parts on one another. This definition of environment also includes human society, which is an integral part of this enormously complex system, also known as the earth system. The following sections provide a brief overview of the most relevant initiatives promoting open access policies to environmental data, particularly from the global and European perspectives. Next, the chapter describes some of the key technological and infrastructural issues that stakeholders in the environmental sector are facing in attempting to implement open access policies to data. Last, it discusses the all-encompassing issue of governance of this highly-heterogeneous landscape, where geo-political, economical, industrial, legal, and institutional issues must all be harmonised in order to enable our society to gain a full picture of the earth system.

Open access and the earth system

Scientific research over recent decades has led to the conclusion that the earth system has been changing outside its range of natural variability, at least in the last half million years, possibly under the influence of human activities (Steffen *et al.* 2004). Such planetary-scale changes in the earth system, including large-scale changes in society, are referred to as 'global change', so the environmental sector illustrates the importance of open data to benefit society.

In fact, global change is posing unprecedented difficulties to decision and policymakers, because strategic goals for globally-sustainable development need to be agreed upon at a planetary level. To enable measuring, monitoring and assessing of these strategies and policies, we need shared indexes based on sound environmental and socio-economic indicators that, in turn, originate from fundamental physical variables and hence, ultimately, from data.

Nowadays, a fundamental enabler of environmental research practice is space-based earth observation. Many international bodies (e.g. those participating in the United Nations Conference on Sustainable Development in 2012) recognise that earth observation from space is key to addressing global change, as also testified by the significant investments availed in this so far. These have demonstrated a positive return across a wide range of societal benefit areas akin to environmental monitoring, such as humanitarian aid, increasing food security, crime prevention and disaster management. However, the high costs involved mean that no single country, programme or industry can undertake this daunting endeavour alone. Instead, the whole of human society needs to be engaged and mobilised, in both developed and developing countries. In fact, developing countries often face an extremely difficult dilemma between preserving their natural resources and industrialisation; hence, their impact on the environment may be very significant.

Understandably, in this context, the sharing of data, resources and knowledge is considered more of an opportunity than a liability. In fact, several global initiatives are pursuing data sharing and capacity-building efforts, including the United Nations Office for Outer Space Affairs (UNOOSA), which aims to bring the benefits of space technologies for sustainable development in an equal way to the broadest spectrum of nations. As Director Simonetta Di Pippo notes:

> although more and more satellites are launched into space almost weekly by a growing number of space-faring nations, and in spite of the rapid growth in cooperative efforts, only a small percentage of the over 200 countries in the world have adequate access or capacity to work with space-based technologies and data, due to technological or resource limitations and often a lack of capacity awareness. (Di Pippo 2014).

Open data could be a true enabler and a formidable asset for decision makers in developing countries, which typically lack the most sophisticated technology and expensive infrastructures required for space-based applications. Di Pippo praises the fact that 'visionary programmes such as *Landsat* paved the way for a large amount of space-based data to be released into the public domain,' and that 'a few visionary private entities in particular in the last ten years have made space-based data accessible to the public through their significant investments into the accessibility of satellite imagery and applications, permitting greater familiarity with the availability and benefits of space-based data' (*Ibid.*). Google Earth is a remarkable example of this. Di Pippo continues: 'If there is a more equal playing field in terms of access to space-derived data, it is thanks to strategic and crucial decisions to make the data public. This has led to a growing interest and demand for training on how to work with such data and on how to derive information from it for more informed decision-making and for varied uses' (*Ibid.*).

The environmental sector is also of particular interest because it is naturally interrelated with two important points of contact between science and technology and society: that of public sector information (PSI) and big data. The public sector is one of the main advocates of open access policies, and provides many examples of successfully implementing open data environmental management policies, in publications and research or government data. Meanwhile, the 'big data revolution' predicted by policymakers in Europe and beyond is having a significant impact on the governance of public resources, and is bringing about novel ways of addressing environmental challenges, as the European Commission's (EC) Digital Agenda for Europe (DAE) recognises (EC 2016a).

Since the environment is part of the earth system, environmental data can be considered a subset of geospatial data, as they are both geographic and spatial in nature, and typically characterised by their position relative to the earth. This chapter refers to geospatial data gathered from earth observation to illustrate the implications of accessing such data in conjunction with open policies.

The environmental data ecosystem

As the World Wide Web Consortium (W3C) and Open Geospatial Consortium noted in a recent collaboration agreement (W3C 2015), spatial data is ubiquitous and integral to many human endeavours. Therefore, making spatial data easier to access and use can be extremely valuable. For example, in the United States alone, geospatial data and services are estimated to generate $1.6 trillion annually (Henttu *et al.* 2012). At the level of the global environmental movement, scientists, governments, policymakers and activists widely support the use of open data.

This generalised sense of consensus has helped stakeholders to mobilise some level of open data within the wider environmental community. In addition, efforts to strengthen the political cohesion of geographical regions (e.g. the European Union), to digitise public administration, to better understand and mitigate global scale phenomena (e.g. climate change), and the growing interest in spatial exploration programmes, are all greatly contributing to the momentum of the open data movement in the environmental sector.

One of the main advocates of open data in the geospatial sector is the Group on Earth Observation (GEO no date), a global voluntary group comprising over 100 nations and more than 90 international participating organisations such as UNOOSA. GEO promotes information sharing across many different scientific disciplines and applications, by providing a coordinated and sustained observation framework with a global and flexible network of content providers (which currently interconnects more than 130 autonomous infrastructures) – the Global Earth Observation System of Systems (GEOSS) – which gives decision makers direct access to an extraordinary range of data and information.

The GEO explicitly acknowledges the importance of data sharing in achieving the societal benefits they anticipate from GEOSS: 'The societal benefits of Earth observations cannot be achieved without data sharing' (GEO 2005). Thus, the GEOSS implementation plan sets out a set of data sharing principles for exchanging data, metadata, and products:

–   There will be full and open exchange of data, metadata and products shared within GEOSS, recognising relevant international instruments and national policies and legislation.

- All shared data, metadata and products will be made available with minimum time delay and at minimum cost.
- All shared data, metadata and products, being free of charge or no more than the cost of reproduction, will be encouraged for use in research and education (*Ibid.* p.8).[1]

Conceding that these data sharing principles may remain an abstract goal until all parties (members, contributors, users) can appreciate how they will implement them, The GEO devised an action plan, which identifies some of the negative implications of open access for environmental data in the GEOSS context (GEO 2010). A primary negative implication is of a financial nature. Various data providers perceive that enabling a full and open exchange of data, metadata and products in GEOSS could pose challenges to their own development which would result in limited revenue, particularly as payments for reuse contradict the GEOSS data sharing principles. Furthermore, many providers cannot visualise a business model that would work if they adopted the principle of full and open exchange of data. Yet, in many cases, requiring users to pay for access to data impedes its use, especially if acquiring the necessary funding to purchase data is a long and arduous process. Hence, the data providers can only realise very limited societal benefits if the product is not attractive, and easily accessible, to the users. To rectify the above and to mitigate providers' reluctance to share their data and products openly, the action plan suggests that the GEO community should demonstrate how the full and open exchange of data can lead to new applications, additional jobs and more open competition, in contrast to the old model of data protection. One action taken to achieve this goal is the GEO 'Appathon', a global app development competition that aims to develop new, exciting and (most importantly) useful applications using earth observation data (GEO 2014).

Another negative implication of open access is that different disciplines, sectors and countries have developed different socio-cultural approaches to open data in the environmental sector, resulting in language barriers and different rates of development in countries across the globe. The GEO recognises that a commonly-endorsed vision is needed to bridge these gaps and overcome such barriers. Incompatibilities between different countries' legal frameworks are also seen as inhibitors that need to be adapted, in

---

1   In GEOSS terms, 'full' and 'open' are interpreted as 'taking into account international instruments and national policies and legislation', whereas 'minimum cost' is interpreted as 'free or cost of reproduction'.

order to remove legal barriers that could slow the implementation of the GEOSS data sharing principles. In some cases, the principle of full and open exchange of data is inconsistent with current national policies. The GEO tries to address this issue by encouraging both national and international bodies to adopt the principle of full and open exchange of data.

The GEO appreciates that it is important to recognise such negative implications, in order to mitigate them. For example, paying for data may not only hinder their use because of the price, but also because the mechanisms for paying are too cumbersome. In fact, barriers to data access are not simply a matter of pricing policies, but also include the varying policies across data providers and countries, so that negotiating access with each provider is extremely complex and long, thus creating a de facto barrier.

At the European level, on 3 March 2010, the European Commission proposed the framework for the 'Europe 2020' initiative (EC 2016b), a ten-year strategy to advance the European Union's economy. The first of seven Europe 2020 flagship initiatives, the Digital Agenda for Europe (DAE) (EC 2016a) contains a specific policy on open data (EC 2016c), including legislation on the reuse of government data (EC 2015), such as the Directive on Access to Public Sector Information (EC 2003a), which applies to any data held by public authorities.

There is also an emphasis on open government data policy (as discussed in Chapter Three) in this area, which is implemented by the Public Sector Information Directive. Open government data is at the centre of a cluster of initiatives within various EC policy domains, which build on and complement the open data policy. One example is the European Commission Communication on Marine Knowledge 2020 (EC 2010a), which aims, amongst other things, to make marine data easier and less costly to use. Other areas impacted by the open government data policy include transport systems, scientific research and cultural heritage. In addition, the gradual deployment of the EC open data policy is expected to have an impact on a number of domains that do not yet have concrete open policies, but which will undoubtedly profit from the benefits of opening up a wide range of public and business data across areas such as education, tourism, consumer protection and public health.

EC environmental policy initiatives are founded on the Directive on Public Access to Environmental Information (EC 2003b), based on the Aarhus Convention (UNECE 1998), and have the most solid links to the open data policy. A remarkable example of this is the INSPIRE Directive (EC 2007), which aims to achieve the widest possible harmonisation and sharing of environmental information throughout the European Member States.

Article 17(1) of the 'INSPIRE Directive' requires each member state to adopt measures to share spatial datasets and services between its public authorities, in relation to public tasks that may have an impact on the environment. Since most of these EC institutions and bodies have to integrate and assess spatial information from all the member states, INSPIRE acknowledges the need to be able to gain access to, and use spatial data and spatial data services in accordance with an agreed set of harmonised conditions.

The main points of the INSPIRE Regulation (EC, 2010b) are that:

- Metadata must include conditions which apply to access and use for EC institutions and bodies; this will facilitate their evaluation of the available specific conditions, even at the discovery stage.
- Member states are requested to provide access to spatial data sets and services without delay – within 20 days on receipt of a written request at the latest, although mutual agreements may allow an extension of this standard deadline.
- If data or services can be accessed under payment, EC institutions and bodies are entitled to ask member states to provide information on how these charges have been calculated.
- While fully safeguarding the right of member states to limit sharing – when this would compromise the course of justice, public security, national defence or international relations – member states are encouraged to find the means to give access to sensitive data under restricted conditions, (e.g. providing generalised data sets). Upon request, member states should give reasons for their limitations on sharing.

As regards public access to data and services supplied under INSPIRE, the EC guidance document states that, if no provisions are contained in the agreement between member states and the EC institutions and bodies, then access given should be guided by whether public access is already, or could be, allowed in the member state and under what conditions (EC 2013a). Public access should therefore be promoted as much as possible, while respecting any exemptions provided for by law. When this public access to spatial data sets or services cannot be allowed, due to an exemption provided for by law, data producers are encouraged to state the conditions under which such access would be possible, for example by removing sensitive information, downgrading the accuracy or restricting the size of the download. It also suggests that any such measures should be harmonised, as far as possible, within and between member states, so that they can effectively be applied to aggregated data sets that might, potentially, come from a large number of producers.

INSPIRE establishes a list of topics that it considers particularly critical for successful data and service sharing within and between member states, supplying criteria for good practice in each. For example, it defines public access as: 'the ability of the public to discover, view and download information and data and to use available services and data. [...] The public authorities should make their data and services available in a way that makes it easy for the citizen to obtain access. It states that usage conditions and charges should be presented in an understandable way' (INSPIRE 2013, p. 46). The following criteria characterise good practice in public access:

–   Awareness by the public that data and services exist – the public knows where it can find data and services, i.e. there is a central portal with registries and search engines that allow citizens to find out where they should go to obtain access to data or services. Awareness-raising activities are also promoted through other means (e.g. flyers). Increasing public awareness will usually be reflected by the growth in use of such websites.

–   A clear process for the public to access data and services – the public authorities provide clear and user-friendly information on how citizens can obtain access to data and services and under which conditions and charges. This information is also provided online, with contact details for obtaining more information.

–   Online access wherever possible – citizens can also obtain access to data online rather than via paper or digital copies, on CD or consultation on site (*Ibid.*).

Data mobilisation at the European level is exemplified by Copernicus, previously known as Global Monitoring for Environment and Security (GMES), which is the main European programme for establishing capacity for earth observation (Copernicus 2016). Copernicus is a European system for monitoring the earth, which collects data from multiple sources, processes these data, and provides users with reliable and up-to-date information related to environmental and security issues. The main users of Copernicus's services are policymakers and public authorities needing sufficient information to develop environmental legislation and policies, or to take critical decisions in the event of emergencies such as natural disasters or humanitarian crises.

Copernicus covers six thematic areas: land; marine; atmosphere; climate change; emergency management; and security. These support a wide range of applications, including environment protection; management of urban areas; regional and local planning; agriculture; forestry; fisheries; health; transport; climate change; sustainable development; civil protection;

and tourism. The architecture of Copernicus comprises in-situ stations (airborne, seaborne and ground-based sensors) and a space component that consists of both missions contributed by members (e.g. commercial or national satellites) and dedicated satellite missions, such as the Sentinel constellation. The space component also includes services to facilitate access to the massive amount of data and information expected from Copernicus, which will be many times more than the volume of data produced by the Sentinel-1, -2, -3 A-series, which is roughly equivalent to 25 Envisat missions (ESA 2012), or over 25 petabytes of data (Laur 2012).

Based on the Copernicus services and on the data collected through the Sentinels and contributing missions, many value-added services can be tailored to specific public or commercial needs, resulting in new business opportunities. In fact, several economic studies have already demonstrated a huge potential for job creation, innovation and growth. This is a major positive outcome expected from Copernicus, in terms of strengthening earth observation markets in Europe. In particular downstream actors, i.e. those developing products and services based on this data, should experience growth and job creation. European research, technology and innovation communities will also be supported in making the best use of these data to create innovative applications and services (Koch 2014).

As a strategic pan-European programme requiring significant resource investment, Copernicus is coordinated and managed by the European Commission, in cooperation with the European Space Agency (ESA) for the space element, and the European Environment Agency (EEA) and the member states for the in-situ component. The member states and the European Parliament have mandated the EC to define Copernicus's overall data and information policy, whose basic principle is full and open access to all data and information produced by services and collected through Copernicus infrastructure, including the Sentinel missions.

The Sentinel data policy was jointly agreed by the EC and ESA (European Space Agency, *Sentinel-2 Preparatory Symposium*, April 2012, slide 9; cited in Desnos 2013), based on joint principles prepared in 2009 (ESA 2009). The policy has been implemented by the Copernicus regulation (European Parliament and the Council 2014), which replaces the previous regulation on the initial operations (2011 to 2013) of GMES (European Parliament and the Council 2010). The Copernicus regulation implies a commitment to follow the GEOSS data sharing principles. In fact, the Copernicus policy promotes the access, use and sharing of data and information on a completely full, free and open basis. To understand the extent of this freedom, it is interesting to highlight the key general provisions of Copernicus' data and information policy:

- No restriction on use, including reproduction, redistribution, and adaptation, for commercial and non-commercial purposes; in particular, no difference is made between public, commercial and scientific use.
- All datasets, including the Sentinel data, are always available on the Copernicus dissemination platform free of charge (or at the minimum cost of fulfilling the user requests).
- Worldwide access to data for European and non-European users, without any limitation in time.

Security restrictions and licensing conditions, including registration, may limit these general principles. For example, access limitations are foreseen for conflict of rights, where the Copernicus open dissemination affects Intellectual Property Rights (IPR) from third parties and principles recognised by the Charter of Fundamental rights of the European Union. Other limitations may apply for security reasons, where the Copernicus open dissemination may affect the security of EU member states, or for urgency. In every case, the decision must be balanced between protecting security interests and the social benefits of open dissemination.

While no warranty is given on the data and information provided, the policy only imposes one obligation, which is an attribution clause, the need to cite the source of data and declare any modification that is made. Regarding user identification, the policy allows quasi-anonymous use, specifying that there should be no need for users to register to access and view services, and only a light registration for use of the download service. It is worth noting that data generated by missions contributed to by Copernicus members, such as commercial or national satellites, as well as in-situ data, are considered external to Copernicus, and therefore they are not covered by the policy. However, Copernicus follows or negotiates the rules set by the data providers for such external data.

Another fundamental contribution to the promotion of open data culture is the advent of data journals, a relatively recent addition to the panorama of scientific literature in the environment sector, and beyond. Although data journals are not open access per se, most of them adhere to the open access paradigm, since their main objective is to provide a formal way of publishing data as a citeable entity, similar to research articles in the scholarly literature. This is in contrast to simpler data-sharing approaches, where data producers make data available on a website. A data paper can be seen as an eloquent and readable version of metadata, which describes a dataset, including its purpose, scope, coverage, format, provenance and quality. Tools are already available to create data papers directly from existing metadata, such as the GBIF Integrated Publishing Toolkit (Robertson *et al.* 2014). Importantly, a data paper has a unique persistent identifier (PI) assigned to it, which ensures that it can be identified and cited. This means that data producers can now receive credit for their work, which is expected to incentivise data publication. Some examples of environmental data journals are the Earth System Science Data (Copernicus), the *Geoscience Data Journal* (Wiley), the *Biodiversity Data Journal* (Pensoft), and the Data Papers of the Ecological Archives (ESA). More generic data journals include *Scientific Data* (Nature), *Data Science Journal* (CODATA/ICSU), and *GigaScience* (BioMed Central).

Open environmental data: Key technological and infrastructural issues

The main role of the technical infrastructure is to provide uniform and equal access to the broad variety of research outputs, i.e. making data understandable, searchable, retrievable, available, assessable and secure. Our work on the RECODE project highlighted five main key technological and infrastructural challenges that stakeholders in the environmental sector face in mobilising their data: heterogeneity, accessibility, sustainability, quality and security.

Heterogeneity relates to the different ways of formatting, storing and using the variety of data available from a growing number of disparate sources. It comprises low-level issues such as format encoding and interoperability of the communication protocols as well as higher-level matters such as application interoperability, semantics mismatches, cross-disciplinary usability, internationalisation, and discoverability – that is how easy it is for users to find the data they need.

Accessibility relates to the volume of data and its impact on the infrastructure's capabilities and architecture. Data volume is a storage matter and becomes a processing issue when data must be analysed. Hence, this challenge is connected to the big data aspects of volume and velocity, in relation to data streaming, record structures, organisation of storage and processing resources, data indexing, filtering and delivery. Velocity concerns both how quickly data is produced, and how quickly data must be processed to meet demand, with related bandwidth issues arising from the huge amounts of data being stored and accessed.

The adoption of open standards helps to both mitigate heterogeneity and improve accessibility. Reinforcing the importance of metadata and data standardisation (e.g. defining common models and encodings) promotes ease of deposit and retrieval for stakeholders such as researchers, universities, libraries and the general public. At the same time, data variety is inevitable, to some extent, so should be acknowledged and accommodated, using distributed architectures and interoperability solutions to fill the gaps between existing systems. Good practice advocated by the system-of-systems[2] approach and brokering or mediation solutions should be considered, as adopted, for example, in GEOSS, where the infrastructure is able to provide harmonised discovery and access services to heterogeneous data by using a brokering approach (Nativi *et al.* 2012). An infrastructure for open access to research data should be conceived as a system-of-systems, to leverage existing infrastructures, supplementing rather than supplanting them, to protect previous investment, guarantee sustainability, and ensure valuable participation from the whole research community.

Sustainability relates to the long-term impact of maintaining and operating an open infrastructure for research data, in relation to obsolescence, governance of updates and upgrades, data preservation and curation, persistence, scalability and energy footprint. Given the ever-growing amount of data, an increasingly pressing question is what data should be preserved, for how long and in what format (for example, online or offline). These decisions are context-specific and, in most cases, rather subjective. Some best practices that can improve sustainability include virtualisation technologies and periodical migrations to more recent technological solutions (through format conversion, transcoding, etc.) as well as using persistent identifiers. There is also the potential to outsource data curation and preservation to third-party archives (see, for example, DANS 2016), which suggests that the new professional roles and skills required to achieve open access to research data should be investigated. Data management culture is well established in some contexts, such as libraries, and some fields of science (e.g. physics or social sciences), but is almost absent in others, for instance in the wider administrative sector.

Quality denotes the technological support required to evaluate data suitability and appropriateness in relation to data accuracy, completeness, documentation (including metadata and other ancillary information), assessment, validation and peer review, usefulness and fitness for purpose. Quality is a crucial aspect throughout the whole data lifecycle. In the big data realm, it is typically referred to as veracity and is conceived as an indication of data integrity, including trustworthiness, provenance,

2   For a definition of 'system-of-systems' see Dersin 2015.

accuracy, and certainty. To address the quality challenge, it is necessary to enforce the presence of complete and accurate metadata, by requiring data producers and disseminators to provide and maintain appropriate ancillary information when publishing and curating their data. This should also comprise tools to auto-generate provenance information, manage versions, and enable data creators, providers and users to assess data quality. However, this is often perceived as being too onerous. To mitigate this sensitive issue, several data-sharing initiatives (e.g. GEOSS) advocate adopting the concept of fitness for use, which seems more neutral than quality. This could be implemented by supporting the collection of user feedback in data repositories, which could be integrated with the metadata to assist users in assessing the suitability of data for their specific purpose.

Security concerns restrictions on the usage, access and consultation of data and metadata as well as their enforcement from a technical viewpoint, e.g. protocols for authentication, authorisation and auditing or accounting, privacy issues and licensing. Technical challenges related to security mainly arise from the variety of data policies, licences, embargo periods, specific IPR, privacy and legal issues that need to be considered when building data infrastructures. For example, some disciplines deal with sensitive data that should be obfuscated (e.g. the location of endangered species), while others manage data under specific licences (e.g. academic programmes for commercial remote-sensing data vendors), where only derived data products can be shared. In other cases, data is withheld until the research project ends or an embargo period expires. Hence, a security framework for authentication, authorisation and auditing is a mandatory component for most data infrastructures in the environmental sector. A good practice is to enforce data policies automatically, where possible, using approaches like 'privacy by design', which designs privacy and data security protections into systems at the outset rather than relying on costly retro-fits. Furthermore, it is important to recognise that sharing does not necessarily mean unrestricted and free access. A common practice is to make metadata immediately available for discovery, with the underlying data only being published after a certain time.

All five of these aspects of the complex open access ecosystem are mutually interrelated. To effectively allow researchers to identify, evaluate, access and use relevant scientific information extracted from a variety of sources, in a variety of formats, it is necessary to recognise the importance of semantic and multidisciplinary interoperability and to adopt technical and infrastructural solutions that holistically address data harmonisation, preservation and technological obsolescence as well as data documentation and metadata, quality and relevance indicators and security aspects.

Despite this, there is a clear tendency in the open data debate to refer to science as a whole sector, ignoring the differences between disciplines in further policymaking. In reality, though, each discipline has different methods for gathering and analysing data, which may be visual, numerical, narrative or statistical, presented in small, medium or large data sets, discrete or interlinked. Moreover, the definition of research data includes public sector information. This implies an essential, inherent heterogeneity. Any policy for open access to research data should therefore take a flexible approach, applying adaptable technological and organisational solutions, and avoiding approaches that do not satisfy the specifics of different disciplinary communities, and thereby raise entry barriers that are already high, and growing.

RECODE research has also highlighted that technical barriers are considered to be more a concern in the environmental sector than cultural ones. This suggests that the acceptance of open access in environmental sciences could be limited more by technology than by stakeholders' willingness to share their data. However, technological and infrastructural hindrances are not perceived as a key obstacle to achieving the adoption of open access to research data, when compared to financial, political, ethical and legal issues, and all of the administrative and process-oriented elements of data management, which is generally referred to as data governance.

Issues in open data governance

Although the environmental sector is witnessing a general push towards abandoning the traditional model of data protection, in favour of a full and open exchange of data, in the belief that this will lead to new applications, additional jobs and more open competition, the major obstacles in relation to open data governance are:

- Interoperability, due to the large heterogeneity of applications, languages, policies, and legal frameworks characterising the context.
- Financial, given the investments required for earth observation, and the industrial sector's determination to protect their investments and competitiveness. This includes the need for one or more effective and sustainable business models characterising the open data process, and open science more generally.
- Curation and preservation, which are related to the previous two challenges, because a sustainable business model is required to guarantee data and related software interoperability over long periods, for instance, for longitudinal climate change research.

As already mentioned, many of the infrastructural and technological issues in open access to research data relate to those typical of big data. With the advances in satellite technology, the future ubiquity of sensors and the uptake of crowdsourced approaches, it is reasonable to expect a growing overlapping between open access and big data issues, particularly around the sharing, preservation and curation of research data. As big data and open access concerns coincide, and open data repositories become more immense, their governance will become an increasingly pressing concern. The current trend may lead to a bureaucratisation of governance, where critical decisions are delegated to politicians who are, typically, not fully aware of the related scientific implications. It is preferable that the governance of big open access repositories primarily involves scientists, who should eventually use them to advise policymakers about critical decisions.

One concern about open data governance is the way that the increasing momentum of open access is spurring on a significant number of volunteer efforts into data sharing in diverse contexts, which is resulting in data sharing solutions being implemented at very different scales, e.g. for a single community of practice or specific project, and in the fragmentation of data into a puzzle of individual pieces, which may be referred to as 'semi-open data pools', or 'semi-commons' (Reichman *et al.* forthcoming). Although, in principle, these are informed by the overall vision of data sharing, they actually work in isolation from each other. To mitigate this problem, funders may oblige publishers to publish data as open access, together with scientific articles, or force them to transfer their semi-commons data into open access repositories, when the projects cease to exist. Another issue is how to combine data that fall under different jurisdictions, e.g. EU and USA policies, especially when such a combination of data is suitable for commercial exploitation. Funders and policymakers should address this problem, for example by developing standard data transfer licences that may be automatically enforced at the infrastructural and technological level.

The Copernicus data policy itself provides an insight into the problems connected to open data governance. The fact that the Copernicus policy is supported by a regulation has both positive and negative implications: on the positive side, as a formal normative document, it could be aligned with other relevant directives, such as the EU INSPIRE Directive 2007/2/EC and the EU PSI Directive 2003/98/EC. This facilitates the consistent implementation of open access in the environmental sector throughout the whole EU. On the other hand, as a formal EU regulation, its provisions are legally binding for European entities, but they cannot have the same efficacy on foreign entities outside the EU. In particular, the principle of worldwide (European and non-European users) access, without limitation in time, coupled with the absence of restrictions on the purpose of use (including commercial exploitation) has raised major concerns, particularly by the European industrial sector, about indirect negative implications for competitiveness. Among other concerns, industry has expressed the view that granting free access to Copernicus data and information to non-European entities, including those from countries such as China and India, which have less expensive cost structures, may result in them gaining a competitive advantage over European industry.

To counteract this problem, clear criteria to define targeted users, their legal status and origin in order are being determined, to ensure that implementing the Copernicus data policy will not reduce the European market share of the earth observation industry. Industry representatives have therefore asked the European Commission to review the current version of the Copernicus data policy and consider introducing limitations on data access for non-European entities, particularly for for-profit entities and their commercial use of Copernicus data and services.

The European Commission is analysing this request and the potential legal and policy impacts arising from measures that would restrict the principle of full, free and open access to Copernicus data and information for non-EU commercial entities. On 27 September 2013, the Committee on Industry, Research and Energy (ITRE) submitted a draft proposal amendment on the Copernicus regulation. In particular, the report submitted that Article 14 of the Copernicus regulation should be amended as follows:

> Copernicus data and information shall be made available on a full, open and free-of-charge basis for all participating Member States, for emergency situations and for development aid purposes. In all other cases a policy of pay-for-data shall be adopted or a reciprocity principle shall be applied (ITRE 2013).

However, the issue is very complicated and it is likely that both industry and ITRE proposals on potential restrictions in accessing and using Copernicus data and information for non-EU entities could lead to a violation of EU obligations and commitments under the WTO General Agreement on Trade in Services (GATS) (Amedeo and Baumann 2013). This example illustrates the fact that addressing these problems requires all the parties involved to agree on mutual policies on the exchange, sharing, access and use of interoperable data and services across various levels of public authority and different sectors of society, at a global level.

The work of the Research Data Alliance (RDA) on middleware governance is of particular interest in understanding the most important challenges to governing and sustaining a digital infrastructure, and to share data sets that are not necessarily from a single community (RDA no date). Effective middleware governance has the potential to support longer-term development under a variety of funding models, to simplify and standardise access models, and to establish a basis to ensure sustainable, stable development and effectiveness in an operational environment. The RDA identifies the following main challenges for achieving effective and sustainable open data governance:

- Secure financial support – the efforts required to obtain and sustain funding. This may include proposal writing, obtaining venture capital, reporting, etc.
- Engage user communities – the efforts required to identify, target, engage and sustain a class of institutional and/or disciplinary and cross-disciplinary science users and their data facilities.
- Marketing – the effort required to understand requirements and then pursue the case(s) for commitment to using a shared capability. This is focused on individual users or facilities and moves beyond the general engagement of a user community.
- Human resources – the personnel support and expertise required for market development, management and achieving the technical capability for infrastructure evolution and sustainment.
- Software engineering – the effort, including formal and informal processes, required to provide development and ongoing maintenance, improvement and technology assessment of software assets.
- Product management – the management of documentation, versions, licensing, distribution, security and other administrative activities.

If necessary, the legal considerations of operating in a multinational or global environment must be added. The RDA study considers the following possible business models for achieving good open data governance:

- Government funding through assistance awards and contracts.
- Government funding through data facility guardianship.
- Software as a service (SaaS).
- Information and advertising sales.
- Corporate support and product or service sales.
- Consortia.

Naturally, each of these has advantages and weaknesses. Although business revenue and/or hybrid models for sustainability can be identified, these approaches will be most successfully applied to the research community when they are amended to fit specific community cultures and practices. Therefore, the RDA study identifies the following community best practice which can be used to shape the most effective governance and business models:

- Low cost.
- Open source, which
  - promotes stakeholder engagement
  - reinforces community practices and standards
  - may promote interoperability standards across communities
  - may mitigate volunteer fatigue
- Community-driven development and evolution.

Conclusion

The environmental sector illustrates several implications of accessing data in conjunction with open policies, in particular regarding data stemming from earth observation, where a big data revolution is predicted. The increasing availability of multidisciplinary data from new observation platforms is expected to provide scientists and society with unprecedented resources through which to understand our planet and better control or mitigate the environmental dynamics. In turn, a better use of globally-available national and local data sets will enable policymakers to make informed and evidence-based decisions to address global change.

The examples discussed above show that the sector is experiencing a general drive to abandon the traditional model of data protection, in favour of full and open exchange of data, in the belief that this will lead to new applications, additional jobs and more open competition. However, despite this obvious mobilisation and the significant gains in achieving agreement and cooperation on key issues, key challenges remain. The major challenges of open environmental data sharing can be identified as interoperability issues, due to the significant heterogeneity of technologies, applications, languages and legal frameworks characterising the context as well as financial concerns, given the investments required for earth observation and the industrial sector's determination to protect their investments and global competitiveness.

Addressing these problems requires mutually agreed policies on the exchange, sharing, access and use of interoperable data and services across various levels of public authority and different sectors of society, at a global level. Such complexities may be reduced by following some recommendations:

- Build on the existing research infrastructures, to supplement, rather than supplant them, applying flexible and adaptable technological and organisational solutions. This is essential to guarantee sustainability and valuable participation from the research communities. The aim should be to fill the gaps and make the existing research infrastructure interoperable, by mediating, instead of imposing common solutions that may not satisfy each community's specific needs, or even raise already-high barriers to entry.
- Distinguish between different approaches to open access, for instance, acknowledging that sharing does not always mean giving away for free.
- Discuss new business models that can sustain the open data approach (e.g. evolving governance and business models based on public-private partnerships).
- Leverage the experience and lessons learned from ongoing national, European and international initiatives such as INSPIRE, GEOSS and Copernicus.
- Discuss new professional roles and curricula which specialise in data science, and open data in particular.

In summary, to overcome the technological barriers of open research data access, there should be a particular focus on the problem of data discovery and access, of analytical search tools and techniques involving aspects such as the use of metadata, relevance indicators, key word searches and third-party recommendations, to help researchers and the public find their way through the mass of scientific information and research data, to identify the material that best fits their purpose. The problems of technological sustainability and obsolescence should also be considered, because these related issues have specific impacts on ensuring continued, sustained access to research data over time. Successful and emerging technologies that can be optimised to provide better access to scientific information and research data should be identified, including technological solutions that are being used in open access repositories, to identify which approaches might be replicated to increase interconnections between scientific information and research data repositories across Europe.

Metadata, particularly provenance information, are of paramount importance in ensuring the repeatability of processes, and good open standards would facilitate a culture of information sharing. The importance of metadata and data standardisation should be reinforced by, for example, agreeing on common models and encodings, to promote the ease of deposit and retrieval for stakeholders including researchers, universities, libraries and members of the public.

Nonetheless, the approach to open research data in Europe should take account of the diverse attitudes in different fields of science towards the issue, as well as the specificities of different communities, which means that there is always an inherent heterogeneity. Therefore, data heterogeneity should be acknowledged and accommodated, by the use of distributed interoperability solutions between existing systems, to enable access to heterogeneous content via the usual platforms. To this end, system-of-systems and mediation solutions may be adopted, following the example of GEOSS, where the infrastructure is able to provide harmonised discovery and access to heterogeneous data by means of a brokering approach. In addition, the cultural changes needed to foster open access to environmental data are much bigger than the technical challenges. This holds true, in particular, for communities that do not require cutting-edge technology to perform their routine research tasks. In fact, communities that are limited by technology typically help to push technological boundaries and advance in terms of data mobilisation and sharing.

Providing open access to data is still at an early stage within Europe and internationally, and its impacts on the creation of a knowledge society are only beginning to be determined. Along with the lessons learned from more widespread open access in publications, the experience gained by global information sharing endeavours in the environmental sector, such as GEOSS, offer a useful insight into the challenges, suggest some possible solutions, and provide valuable experience and good practice to reflect on, when discussing strategies for the future. Nevertheless, this case study demonstrates that, even in a relatively bounded, although heterogeneous, discipline, where the benefits of information sharing are obvious and generally accepted by stakeholders, and where significant gains in working out issues related to institutions, legal frameworks and standards have been made, there are still many obstacles to be overcome to enable the sharing of data to significantly contribute to a knowledge society, even within earth observation itself. This indicates that much work remains to suitably leverage open access to data to achieve all of the potential benefits foreseen from this opening.

8. Navigating legal and ethical frameworks

Introduction

In many contexts, ethical, legal and social issues have been discursively constructed as a barrier or challenge to providing open access to data, especially data that raises intellectual property or privacy and data protection issues. However, others have argued that providing open access to data, especially data resulting from publicly-funded research, is also an ethical imperative. Specifically, it has the potential to 'level the playing field in terms of who has access to information and knowledge' (Sveinsdottir *et al.* 2013, p. 36), 'increase public trust and stimulate business activity' (The Royal Society 2012, p. 7), and 'increase public understanding of science, inspire the young, result in better quality decision making in government and commerce, and bring other benefits' (Dallmeier-Tiessen *et al.* 2012, p. 16). Consequently, alongside the need to meet legal obligations and ethical standards around research and data collection, academic researchers are also being strongly encouraged to enable a realisation of the knowledge society, either through opening up as much data as possible, or by exploiting their data to enable innovation.

As discussed in Chapter Three, this encouragement originates, in particular, from policymakers, funders, research institutions and some civil society organisations within the open data movement. Researchers, data centres and institutions are emerging as the key actors in relation to these (sometimes) competing demands, with these groups often leveraging existing infrastructures, processes or mechanisms – or devising new solutions – to tackle these issues simultaneously. This chapter uses information from the RECODE case study interviews, literature review and legal and ethical issues workshop to examine the interplay between ethical, legal and regulatory frameworks in the provision of open access to research data, in order to enable the knowledge society. The details of these regulatory frameworks are important for assessing the way in which openness as a value can be mobilised and institutionalised. The characteristics of these frameworks are significant in shaping how data can be made open. They have to balance numerous demands in terms of enabling data to be open, but in ways that ensure data protection and the responsible use of data. This relates directly to the arguments made in Chapter Four about openness, which highlight the delicacy of ensuring appropriate conditions for open data in fostering an open knowledge society.

Governance structures

The governance of research via governments, policymakers, funders and institutions integrate all of these intersecting, and sometimes competing, demands, which means that researchers, institutions and data centres are required to actively navigate this challenging landscape. At the governmental level, 'governance' refers to legal or legislative obligations, such as privacy, data protection and intellectual property, which may be mandated by national or supra-national (e.g. European) levels of government. These actors might also issue mandates, recommendations, communications or other policy documents in relation to open data, open access or innovation that require or recommend stakeholders such as funding bodies, institutions, researchers and other organisations to undertake particular steps to enable the knowledge economy. In addition to these governmental constraints, stakeholders may also be subject to policymaking guidance from funders and the institutions that make up their ecosystems (e.g. universities, national libraries, disciplinary societies and others).

National, regional and international laws are the first set of governance frameworks that impact upon the provision of open access to research data, with intellectual property rights, rights to privacy and the protection of personal data being the most significant among these. Intellectual property rights protect works by individuals, groups or organisations that are the result of creativity, innovation, skill or specialist effort (Korn and Oppenheim 2011). Intellectual property rights are governed by intellectual property laws, and the US, Japan and all 28 member states of the European Union are among the members of the World Intellectual Property Organisation (WIPO) and have signed up to the Berne Convention seeking to protect authors' rights over their literary or artistic works. The governing of intellectual property rights in relation to open access to research data references both moral rights and exploitation rights for the researchers or institutions that created, collected or curated the data. These may include rights of attribution and the need to respect the original work's integrity as well as copyright, database rights, trade secrets, patents and licences, along with rights to reproduce, distribute and transform materials. Whilst purely factual material is not protected, copyright may also protect collections of data that are sufficiently original and creative, through database rights (Tysver 2013). In Europe, there is a specific law, the 1996 Database Directive, which provides protection rights for anyone who has invested sufficient effort to produce a new database (De Vries 2012). In the EU, database rights are created automatically, do not have to be registered separately to have effect, and are conferred to the creator's employer (when the action of creation was part of employment). However, identifying who holds rights over research data can be difficult in a number of circumstances, including where research is the result of cooperation between large, international consortia or when the data are a cultural artefact related to a certain group of people.

In addition to intellectual property rights, the right to privacy and the protection of data also govern the management of research data, and each region and country has its own privacy and data protection laws. For example, European Union law includes the right to privacy and personal data protection. Currently, personal data in the EU are protected by domestic law in accordance with the European Data Protection Directive (95/46/EC) (soon to be replaced by the General Data Protection Regulation (2016/679)). In contrast, in the US, privacy and data protection are governed by sectoral laws in health, consumer protection and other areas. The Australian legal framework combines the two approaches. It provides both a national overarching 'information privacy' framework through the Privacy Act (1988), but also provides specific additional – sometimes state-level – legislation for data in particular sectors, such as health and consumer data. Much research data contains information that could be used to identify a person, termed 'personally identifiable information' in United States' legislation, especially health, social science, humanities and biological data. As such, ensuring the anonymity of research participants may make it difficult to provide open access to research data. In addition, opening, preserving and sharing research data may introduce issues related to participant consent for additional, unforeseen research practice as well as data protection rights of correction and erasure; for instance, correcting or erasing a single record from all copies of an existing data set (Finn *et al.* 2014).

Alongside these protections for researchers and members of the public, other governance frameworks seek to open up as much research data as possible. This may include governance via national laws or through national, regional or institutional funding policies that require the provision of open access to research data outside of exceptional circumstances. With regard to the former, the US, Italian, Argentinian, Spanish and Belgian governments have all passed specific decrees, laws or declarations relating to open access to publications. Countries in Latin America, which has long been at the forefront of providing open access to publications, are also exploring legislative possibilities for mandating open access to publications and research data (Adams no date). In Argentina, there is a law that requires institutions in receipt of government funding for research data to provide open access to their publications and primary research data up to five years after collection (*Ibid.*). Similar mandates for providing open access to research data also exist in the US and Ireland. Many of these regulations are enacted through the national funding bodies and explicitly or implicitly reference the Liège model (Rentier and Thirion 2011), whereby only publications saved in open access depositories are eligible for inclusion in official reviews of research. Therefore, researchers who do not conform to open access requirements will find themselves at a disadvantage in terms of potential career progression as well as losing access to future funding. For instance, the Belgian law on open access is administered via Belgium's largest public funder of scientific research, the Fund for Scientific Research, which will only fund researchers who comply with their open data policy.

Although many legal mandates do not yet include research data (except in Ireland, Argentina and the US) many national, regional and institutional funders have already extended their open access mandate to include research data. For example, a 2012 European Commission Communication outlines the steps that the EC will take to ensure better access to scientific information, including publications and data, and provides specific recommendations that European member states should take to complement the EC effort (European Commission 2012a). Specifically, the European Commission is running an open data pilot scheme, where consortia who have been awarded EC grant funding are requested to state whether they will participate in the pilot or not and provide reasons – such as privacy, intellectual property or other factors – if they wish to opt out. The UK's largest and most established funding bodies have committed to similar policies. The Wellcome Trust (Wellcome Trust 2010) and the UK's seven Research Councils (RCUK 2015) all require the submission of open data where possible. In the UK, this effort is complemented by Jisc, a charity that advocates open access to research publications and data (Science Metrix 2013). In Australia, the Australian Research Council does not mandate the provision of open access to research data, but it 'strongly encourages' researchers to maintain and deposit their research data, to enable reuse (Steele 2014). It is important to note that all of these open data policies include the option to exclude data that have sensitivities related to privacy, data protection and intellectual property.

Other institutional governance structures are also shaping the requirements that researchers must adhere to with respect to open access to data.

The first is a growing trend within the academy to use research generated by universities for commercial patents, despite this being a potential contradiction to the stated commitment of universities to generate open knowledge. The second is a similar push by research funders, for example the European Commission, to generate 'exploitable' research results to support the economic growth and competitiveness of the European Union. This element also supports providing more open data, which will enable other organisations to generate economic growth from the use of scientific information. This pressure to convert research into socially and economically useful knowledge, in addition to simply producing and transmitting knowledge, has grown over the last two decades (D'Este and Patel 2007). Many universities now have dedicated offices or departments working on these activities, including the Ohio State University's Technology Commercialization and Knowledge Transfer Office and the Imperial Innovations Investment Fund at Imperial College in London (Finn *et al.* 2014). In addition, the European Commission explicitly advocates a data 'exploitation' agenda in its 'Horizon 2020' framework programme, which encourages applicants and funding recipients to consider how their research results could be commercialised or shared, to allow others to exploit them for commercial and other purposes. Other funding agencies have followed suit by introducing clear commercialisation policies (Harmon *et al.* 2012, p. 6).

Finally, institutions and disciplines also have their own internal governance mechanisms, like institutional review boards, editorial review boards and codes of conduct, which govern research practice in particular institutions or disciplines. These mainly deal with ethical issues, such as research with vulnerable individuals, but they may also provide information about how to handle sensitive personal data, establish informed consent and ensure that research results are obtained legally (a matter of importance in archaeology, for example). Each of these issues impacts upon opening up research data, and adds an additional layer of stakeholders and frameworks through which researchers must navigate in order to effectively manage their data.

Navigating these structures to enable innovation

Like Chapters Five, Six and Seven, this section of the chapter uses data from the case studies in five disciplines studied in the RECODE project – archaeology, bioengineering, environmental sciences, health and clinical research, and particle physics – to demonstrate that, despite these potential tensions, stakeholders are finding novel and creative ways to meet legal, ethical and social obligations whilst providing open access. This section describes the case studies in detail, giving particular attention to the data they were working with, the governance frameworks within which they operated and the ecosystem of stakeholders involved. It outlines the specificities of the legal, ethical, social and regulatory issues encountered in each case study, examining the implications for their stakeholders and ecosystems. The section proceeds by identifying and describing the innovative solutions being used, such as applying licensing frameworks, editorial reviews, access management and non-binding 'soft-law' measures to meet legal and ethical requirements and to facilitate the effective preservation and sharing of data.

Archaeology

Within the archaeology case study, there emerged a need to navigate pressures from different stakeholders around issues like intellectual property, privacy, data protection and commercialisation, whilst providing open access to archaeological data.

First, establishing data ownership can be very difficult, but it is necessary in order to determine copyright and other intellectual property rights. One respondent noted that researchers create the data as 'data', whereas the rights of indigenous people, such as First Nations, Native American or Aboriginal peoples, may actually undermine researchers' or institutions' legal copyright and 'might have very different kind of worldviews and traditions and perspectives and their own legal traditions around intellectual property issues' (Repository manager, archaeology). Making the data openly accessible could undermine the rights of these groups once cultural information is digitally available and widely shared. In addition, the archaeology case study revealed an interesting way in which simply making the data accessible via the internet can have unforeseen and unintended commercial impacts. Specifically, web traffic, especially that resulting from search engines like Google, or other commercial services like Facebook or Twitter, can provide commercially useful information about those who access the data. In fact, 'collecting data about our users seems to be the sort of commodity that is really valuable in this space' (*Ibid.*). In fact, this respondent noted that the way that the open ecosystem implicates this wider group of potentially controversial commercial stakeholders is a relatively unacknowledged issue.

Just like health, archaeological data is often about people and, as such, privacy and data protection are important issues to consider and manage when providing open access to archaeological data. These include, but are not limited to, concerns around data retention, consent and anonymity. While data preservation is a key aspect of the open access movement, ethical research practice in many humanities and social science disciplines often advises the destruction of research data that may contain personal information after it has been used. In addition, obtaining consent from all of the stakeholders who might be impacted by archaeological data can be a major difficulty. For example, data related to religious practice or the discovery of remains potentially implicates large numbers of people who may be difficult to identify and track down in order to gain consent. Finally, anonymisation in this space can be difficult to achieve for two reasons. First, some data relates to whole groups of people while, second, other supporting data necessary for contextualisation or reliability, for example global positioning system (GPS) data can contain – or be easily linked to – personal information.

Bioengineering

The bioengineering case study raised issues around intellectual property rights and privacy alongside open access and commercialisation issues, through the development of open source software as well as data protection rights.

With respect to intellectual property, the need to protect the interests of some private companies can impact the extent to which data and software can be made openly accessible. Universities work 'in both the open source public domain area, as well as working with companies that need to preserve IP around particular areas' (Professor, bioengineering). They build 'interfaces based on that open source software framework where those guides can be tailored to the needs of the particular company and then the company will have ownership of that, that interface' (*Ibid.*). However, at the same time, universities are pushing for open source software to be the default IP stance or, alternatively, for commercialisation, which has particular impacts on the quality and sustainability of the resulting programmes and researchers' motivations to provide open access. A laboratory manager in bioengineering explains:

> So, after a year or two, after the funded has ended and if we haven't actually managed to secure new funding to [...] maintain it, not really add

any novelty, your proposals just aren't competitive. [...] [You have] got a whole lot of people actually using the software, they become dependent on it and you now leave them in the lurch because the software becomes unmaintained, all the effort they have put into adopting software is now wasted. And I think some people are actually discouraged from the software in the first place, because they actually see its unlikely to be maintained in future (Laboratory manager, bioengineering).

In this context, competing pressures from the legal framework, private companies, the university and other researchers all converge to impact upon the extent to which data and software can be made openly accessible. Furthermore, it demonstrates how these different governance structures can create competing demands: between funders who may encourage or require open access or open source material, universities who want to provide commercial services, and researchers who want well-maintained and sustainable software products.

In addition, this case study also highlighted specific challenges around privacy and data protection, given the increasing capabilities of bioengineering modelling techniques and competing pressures around different national governance frameworks. While the physiological modelling focused on seemingly anonymous data, such as images of internal organs, the longevity of that anonymity was being challenged by the technological capabilities. For example, a research manager in the VPH case study noted that modelling software and tools are becoming so detailed and sophisticated that it might be possible to identify someone based on images of, for example, their heart, produced by these techniques. In addition, large, multinational research consortia pose their own unique problems. A representative of the bioengineering case study described how research collaboration between their country and the US meant that the researchers had to navigate their own legislation as well as American medical patient data protection frameworks. This resulted in a significant drain on project resources, because 'someone associated with that project had to familiarise themselves and make sure that all the technologies were set up to protect the data in compliance with those [US] regulations' (Laboratory manager, bioengineering).

Environmental sciences

The environmental sciences case study focused on the Group on Earth Observation System of Systems (GEOSS) (Group on Earth Observations

2014), which is primarily situated within the European Commission's Joint Research Centre (JRC). The GEOSS initiative, and the JRC in particular, contends with challenges from all four of the broad governance issues examined here, mainly because the JRC is a public body and therefore is subject to the European Commission's open access to public sector information mandates.

With respect to intellectual property rights, the GEOSS group encounters various issues associated with providing open access to their data whilst respecting the intellectual property of private bodies *and* ensuring that they do not interfere with commercialisation opportunities of other organisations. In the first instance, the JRC finds that they often have to purchase data from private companies and agree licences, many of which do not allow the JRC to provide open access to the data they hold, whether this be raw data or aggregated, derived data:

> The licensing agreements that we have to sign with these companies limit further reuse [...] So, from this perspective, we are still struggling quite a lot to come up with schemes that allow wider access and more open use of the data that we acquire from private companies (Researcher, earth sciences).

In addition, the JRC is in a difficult location with respect to commercialisation because, as an agency of the European government, it is prevented from interfering in commercial opportunities for companies, despite also being required to open their data in order to enable European companies to create new products and services. This means that the JRC must 'be very careful how we might affect the business in the market,' even though their open access data policy is intended to support 'setting up an application that will be sold on the market' (Researcher, environmental sciences). Thus, European legislation, national and European legal frameworks around intellectual property and commercialisation pressures all converge here in the provision of open access to data held by the JRC.

There are also privacy and data protection issues associated with some geographical data, primarily visual data from satellites, but also data from other sources. For example, visual data can reveal information about how land is being used and the inclusion of geographic information system (GIS) or other navigation details can result in this being considered personal data or personally-identifiable information. This is particularly the case when the data is linked with other information sources – for example, where a data set containing GPS coordinates can be linked to public land records to reveal landowners' identities. Thus, the GEOSS case study demonstrates a need to consider not only the legal frameworks around a particular data set, but also the ways that the data could be linked with other data sources once it is made openly accessible.

Health and clinical research

The legal and ethical issues examined in this case study were complex and diverse, and included issues around intellectual property rights, data protection, privacy, research ethics and commercialisation. Intellectual property rights and database rights, in particular, were often complicated by the diffuse institutions, researchers and individuals implicated within the international ecosystem. Often, specific arrangements were made between those responsible for compiling the database and the researchers seeking to utilise the data contained within it:

> You usually have a project officer on a project who will help to set up all the material transfer agreements. And we usually decide which law will be in place and it's usually wherever the database is held (Legal expert, health).

However, the advent of cloud computing has the potential to further complicate issues associated with database rights, because it can make the location of the information unclear. This suggests significant privacy and data protection issues in addition to IPR, as:

> We can never actually, never guarantee confidentiality of all data, because it could be hacked into and we can't anymore say that your data will be anonymous because that is a nonsense too, because we are able to bring in so many different kinds of data, [...] that the potential for people to be re-identified or distinguished in the data are quite high (*Ibid.*).

Yet, despite these challenges around providing the necessary anonymity to meet privacy and data protection requirements, many research participants want their data to be available, accessible and reused by the same or additional researchers. In contexts where such 'broad consent' is not permitted, then consent to open access can become challenging, where it is not possible to arrange dynamic consent instead (Kaye *et al.* 2011; Solum Steinsbekk

2013). It is difficult to reliably anticipate all of the research purposes to which data will be put, if they are made open access.

This demonstrates how health researchers can be trapped between the need to protect patient confidentiality and researchers' intellectual property rights, and the public interest in making health data accessible and reusable. In fact, improvements in health are one of the main areas where the public expect improvements and innovations from data linking, sharing and reuse to be generated (Donovan *et al.* 2014). Thus, privacy, data protection, intellectual property and open access form a complex, multi-layered web of legal and social obligations that health researchers need to find innovative and novel ways to resolve.

Particle physics

Within the governance structures outlined above, the issues experienced by participants in the physics case study centred on intellectual property issues and the fact that the innovations that enable this data to be collected and analysed impact on the ability to provide meaningful open access to the data. With respect to intellectual property issues, one of the key issues is establishing the ownership of data. A data manager describes the experience of CERN:

> The biggest problem is who actually owns the data. So, the collabora-
> tions; so, this consists of many institutes and people worldwide. They
> think that they own the data. The funding agencies who fund either
> CERN (the now 21 CERN member states) as a whole or specific experi-
> ments (e.g. the US, which is not a member state, but is active in both
> ATLAS and CMS, as well as ALICE), they might think that they own
> the data. And then the lab might think it owns the data. So, I would say
> that has never been unambiguously resolved (Data manager, particle
> physics).

Significantly, the members of these large, multinational consortia are often not subject to the same intellectual property laws as research institutions, and may not share similar expectations around the intellectual property generated by the research. This can impact on agreements about providing open access to the data and the manner in which it is provided. Further-more, as discussed in Chapter Six, while the field of physics has a long history of data sharing, realistically achieving open access to that research data, as mandated by different governments and funding organisations, is particularly problematic. The computing required to adequately analyse the data requires significant resources that are unavailable to researchers and citizen scientists outside of the established disciplinary structure (e.g. access to the LHC computing grid). For example, particle physics is certainly aligned with many of the innovation and commercialisation priorities of their institutions, as the 'technology advancements that resulted from building' one data analysis machine is 'hundreds of times more valuable' than the machine itself (Data manager, physics). However, these innovations are often so specific and technically advanced that they can take years to become well-known by the public. The need to utilise these innovative technologies in order to analyse the data means that physics researchers, their institutions and funding agencies are not able to simultaneously meet many of the ethical imperatives of meaningfully opening their data, given their focus on technical and disciplinary innovation.

Physics researchers are working to work within complex, often international, regulatory frameworks around intellectual property rights that implicate governments, institutions and funding organisations. In addition, they must also consider funding requirements to make their data open access, as well as the expectations of institutions and funders that their innovations will have wider implications for knowledge transfer and innovation beyond their research groups and disciplines. However, the public is often absent from this discipline, as many of the innovations are available within the closed system, rather than forming integrating characteristics (e.g. democratising science) of the knowledge society.

Existing novel solutions

The case studies revealed that, although these issues appear to create potential barriers against providing open access to research data, they can also provide an opportunity for innovation. Many researchers, consortia and institutions studied were already using existing solutions in creative ways to manage both the provision of open access and the different stakeholder concerns that impacted on their open access practice. These practices demonstrate how these intersecting pressures can be managed successfully and suggest that the more appropriate question is about 'how' to navigate these demands, not choosing between which ones to accommodate.

The first solution utilised by researchers and academic practitioners from different disciplines was to use licensing to manage how research data was disseminated and reused. As mentioned in Chapter Three, licensing provides a useful way to address intellectual property issues and academic pressures around commercialisation. Creative Commons (https://creativecommons.org/) is a non-profit-making organisation that provides a set of useful licensing models (the most commonly employed form of licensing), while other resources, such as Open Government Licence (http://www.nationalarchives.gov.uk/doc/open-government-licence/version/3/) provide free and flexible use and reuse of copyright and database right materials. These licences permit creators of research data and/or the repositories in which they are stored to make use of licences to establish clear conditions related to how the research data should be used, including, for example, attributing content to original researchers and observing some restrictions on modifying data. Creative solutions in this area include the JRC's use of a set of 'laundry symbols' to signal they ways in which content can be used, without having to read the licence details. Creative Commons licences work in a similar way, with different icons representing levels of restriction on commercial use, derivatives or a lack of any restrictions. Open Context also recommends the use of licences to provide 'a robust and definitive statement' about how digital content can be utilised. This provides security both for those providing the data and those reusing the data, especially given the lack of international laws or even 'international disciplinary sensibilities' (Editorial reviewer, archaeology). However, open licensing models have yet to be adequately tested in courts, and one legal expert has described them as representing something of a 'Wild West' frontier in intellectual property law.

Editorial review is another popular management practice that aims to steer a course through the legal and ethical issues associated with providing open access to research data. Editorial review utilises existing disciplinary and institutional frameworks and expertise to manage the provision of open access to research data, and can be particularly effective in managing privacy, data protection and intellectual property or commercialisation issues. Crucially, it can free researchers or research teams from having to develop this complex expertise themselves. This mechanism was deployed in the archaeology, environmental sciences, health and clinical research and particle physics case studies, and included examples such as the following:

We have data protection coordinators in each Directorate General at the European Commission, so there is one also in the Joint Research Centre and we work close with them, whenever there is data that contains data that can lead to identification of a physical person. So, we contact the coordinator and then, if it needs be, then he contacts the data protection officer of the European Commission and then he provides us with an opinion (Legal expert, earth sciences).

So, what we do is, before it even goes to open context, our data go through a cleaning process, where the sites are allocated to a grid in the grid system and then we scrub the coordinate data and any data that are considered sensitive by our state partners, which can potentially differ state to state, and then we put it up on open context. So, the only location information relates to our grid (Editorial reviewer, archaeology).

These internal review processes employ dedicated legal experts to ensure that they comply with the legal instruments associated with personal data and intellectual property protection as well as ethical research practice. This internal review process works as an effective mechanism to enable organisations within an open access ecosystem to meet all of their legal requirements when releasing data under an open access regime.

Stakeholders also sought ways to manage or curtail access to certain types of data, or to restrict access to those who had particular professional qualifications, to ensure that their data was treated appropriately. Archaeology, clinical and particle physics data all require some form of professional accreditation or other access management review in order to enable researchers to access data. This professional gatekeeping solution allowed these disciplines to ensure legal and ethical compliance to open access to research data. To do this, they identified specific 'professionals' with relevant expertise in research methods or legal requirements such as confidentiality, privacy, data protection and research ethics. Participants in the health case study also described an approval process, whereby an official 'board' would review a researcher's credentials and their research questions to ensure that they were appropriate to the data to which they were seeking access. This solution ensured that the data was used responsibly and that any potential for misuse was identified and mitigated. It also served as an enforcement mechanism, because individuals who did not use data responsibly might not be 'approved' the next time.

Finally, the use of existing ethical and legal guidance instruments, such as checklists or professional codes of conduct were also employed by the case study participants as a way to assist stakeholders in effectively evaluating their responsibilities. However, while soft-law measures encourage ethical practices and legal compliance, they do not mandate them. An ethical editorial reviewer in the archaeology case study explained the adoption of soft-law measures by their organisation:

> [W]e take a lot of our clues on the ethical front from various journals and other kinds of venues where people publish this kind of material routinely and most journals and publishing houses have ethical guidelines that they follow. And we look to them sometimes for clues, because it's quite similar in many ways (Editorial reviewer, archaeology).

This suggests that existing disciplinary organisations as well as other stakeholders such as publishers, funders, repositories, universities and other institutions, all have a significant role to play in assisting open access stakeholders to deal with legal and ethical issues. This further demonstrates that the realisation that legal and ethical open access to research data requires the involvement of a whole ecosystem of stakeholders, each of whom must be mobilised and incentivised in different ways to play their role in the provision of open access to data.

Challenges for open access

The above discussion illustrates both the complex legal environment within which providing open access to data is being managed and the complex ecosystem of stakeholders involved in this. Each of the case studies revealed how international collaborations, intellectual property considerations and the need to protect personal data create challenges for providing open access to data as mandated by governments, funders and institutions. Furthermore, navigating such a complex environment can be a significant drain on researchers' and institutions' time and budgets, since appropriate expertise needs to be found or developed in order to respond effectively to these intersecting – and sometimes conflicting – obligations.

This challenge becomes additionally complex when all of the different stakeholders and interests involved are taken into account. While funders and governments may wish to encourage researchers and institutions to open as much of their data as possible, institutions and funders are also creating pressures to commercialise innovations. Open access incentives, such as the Liège model can incentivise researchers and institutions to participate in open access activities, but they should not have a detrimental effect on those individuals and organisations that are prevented from participating in open access as a result of other legal obligations. A further layer of complexity is the fact that, while researchers themselves may be under legal obligations to protect certain aspects of their research data (e.g. personal data), research participants may be interested in opening up as much data as possible, to enable innovation. Health is one specific area where patients are often keen for their data to be used and shared widely to advance clinical knowledge, despite containing personal information.

However, the main finding of this chapter is that these challenges are being navigated in innovative ways, often using existing mechanisms. Licensing, especially open licensing, editorial reviews, access management solutions and codes of practice, is essential for managing the provision of open access whilst dealing with other legal and ethical obligations. However, many of these solutions impose some kind of limit or control on the use of data, which runs counter to the definitions of open access which is supported by governments, funders and open data activists. For example, the EC definition of open access is 'free internet access to and use of' publications and data (European Commission 2012b). This implies that no restrictions on the use of data should be implemented, but the reality of the legal and ethical landscape requires researchers, institutions and other innovators to think creatively about how to provide open access whilst simultaneously meeting their legal obligations. This is doubly important when the heterogeneity of data, science and research practice, as discussed in Chapters Six and Seven, are taken into account.

Thus, legal, ethical and regulatory issues provide potential to create opportunities for innovation, rather than a just representing a barrier to open access. While governments, funders and institutions should continue to require protection for intellectual property and personal data rights, it cannot be assumed that this will inevitably hinder the provision of open access. Thus, the aim is to provide *both* open access *and* sufficient protection, not mutually exclusive options. Thus, as foreseen in Chapter Two, open access to data can be both dependent on, and a driver for, technological and social innovation. This may also require government, agency and institutional policymakers to increase the flexibility of their definitions of open access. This would open space for providing *meaningful* open access to data. For example, editing data, utilising firewalls and virtual machines to query data, requiring specific credentials and other access management solutions will enable data to be effectively utilised, despite introducing restrictions on the data itself. This is also relevant to the particle physics case study, where gaining meaningful access to data requires specific skills and computing resources, and providing open access to raw data would be an exercise in futility. Instead, data sharing and preservation is widely accepted, despite deviation from traditional definitions of open access.

However, if this opportunity is not sufficiently acted upon, or stakeholders are not adequately supported to experiment with and devise innovative solutions, then it is possible that these obligations will become barriers. Thus, policymakers need to set aside funds and space for experimentation with novel ways of providing open access to data. Failure to do so could also result in liabilities for researchers, institutions and members of the public, either in terms of legal responsibilities around intellectual property, privacy and data protection, or career liabilities in terms of insufficiencies in ethical research practice or open access to data provision. Providing adequate political and financial support for these and other emerging novel solutions is essential in order to enable the knowledge society.

Conclusion

This chapter has demonstrated that reading legal and ethical obligations as barriers to the provision of open access can result in them becoming barriers in reality. While some stakeholders are encountering complex legal landscapes, others are often finding creative ways to meet all of their legal and ethical obligations. Furthermore, these novel practices are also enabling them to address the (sometimes) competing demands of all of the stakeholders within their own research data ecosystems, including policymakers, funders, institutions, other researchers and members of the public. Thus, the goal should be to provide both robust protections and open access to data. Strong legal protections and ethical practice will foster trust in data practices, institutions and governance structures, which will encourage stakeholders to provide data and then open and share that data. Thus, robust legal and ethical practices must be integrated into governance structures in order for changes in data practice to result in significant changes for the knowledge society. Furthermore, funders and policymakers must provide adequate support for the utilisation of, and experimentation with, innovative solutions for providing adequate protection and open access. Constructing these novel solutions as opportunities and investing in them will result in such robust protections, whereas viewing them as barriers will discourage data sharing and, ultimately, hamper efforts to integrate open data and foster the knowledge society.

This chapter also provides an insight into aspects of the relationship between data and the knowledge economy. First, all different types of

actors within open data ecosystems must be effectively mobilised to foster
creative solutions for complex legal requirements that take advantage of
innovations related to data and drive those innovations forward. They must
be encouraged to own the outcomes of the data-fuelled knowledge society.
Second, open data activists within the open data movement need to consider
moving beyond advocacy in relation to key stakeholders to permeation. The
integration of all the different types of stakeholders and actors necessary to
foster solutions for, and trust within, the open data ecosystem is a mammoth
task that is both social and cultural. These activists and supporters need to
consider how to further leverage new technologies to amplify their message
as well as the messages of those who are experimenting, achieving and
being creative within these spaces.

9. Big data, open data and the commercial sector[1]

Introduction

The previous chapters have outlined how open data can contribute to achieving a knowledge society, and described some challenges that need to be overcome. However, it is evident that the government and academic sectors cannot create a knowledge society within a vacuum. The involvement of the commercial sector, partly – although not exclusively – through the knowledge economy, is an important aspect of ensuring that data-related innovations permeate all aspects of society. In this vein, effective citizen collaboration and co-creation of products and services are dependent on the integration of the commercial sector into the knowledge society.

Yet, while open data is often focused on the government and academic sectors, the integration of the commercial sector in this ecosystem also raises a need to consider developments around big data. Linking different types of open data, proprietary data and big data will generate new opportunities for innovation across the ecosystem based on large, heterogeneous data sets that may also integrate some real-time data. Currently, development of innovation in the commercial sector has been uneven. This is a complex innovation space, and evidence from the Open Data 500 (discussed in detail below) indicates that both large, mature companies and small- and medium enterprises (SMEs) and start-ups[2] have already gained some benefit from open data and big data. Yet, companies situated between SMEs and large, multinational companies are not as visible in this space, and the extent to which they are benefiting is somewhat unclear.

Policymakers and some civil society organisations have been enacting specific policies in an attempt to better support data-driven innovations

---

1   Portions of this chapter rely on research conducted within the Big data roadmap and cross-disciplinary community for addressing societal externalities (BYTE) project funded by the European Commission under grant number 619551.

2   Within policy discourses, SMEs and start-ups are often analogous. SMEs are organisations with less than 250 employees and small annual turnover (approx. less than €50m. Often these are relatively new companies and they represent 90 per cent of all businesses in the EU (http://ec.europa.eu/growth/smes/business-friendly-environment/sme-definition/index_en.htm). Start-ups refer to organisations that have been recently founded, which often happen to be small and have a modest turnover, given their stage of development.

that are based on open data and big data across sectors. While some of these policies are producing benefits in this ecosystem, other policies might be simultaneously introducing complexity and contradiction into these endeavours for some stakeholders. Nevertheless, other policies may be contributing to improving rights protections for members of the public whose data underpin these innovations. Thus, considerable research and policy development is required to truly realise the types of data-driven innovations that are needed to foster a knowledge society.

Big data and innovation

The 'flare' of the term 'big data' has been bright, but brief. While its origins can be traced back to small group discussions in Silicon Valley in the 1990s (Lohr 2013), leading to more popular usage in the early twenty-first century (Laney 2001), it gained real prominence after 2009. While Gartner included big data in its annual publication 'Hype Cycle for Emerging Technologies' in 2014, it had disappeared by 2015 (Gartner 2015). Yet, certain aspects of big data continue to require attention within debates about the knowledge society, principally because of the ways in which it implicates the commercial sector and because of the centrality with which policymakers situate big data within the digital innovation space.

Big data and data-driven innovation remain at the early stage of influencing the commercial sector, but it has significant potential for wider impact. In fact, the 2014 Gartner hype cycle report predicted a five-to-ten-year period before big data would reach its plateau of productivity (Gartner 2014). Despite the disappearance of the term in its 2015 review, Gartner had integrated aspects of what had previously been called 'big data' within numerous other emerging technologies, from autonomous vehicles, to the Internet of Things (IOT) to advanced analytics for self-service delivery (Gartner 2015). Thus, in the commercial sector in particular, big data is increasingly becoming embedded within other socio-technical commercial processes and contributing to transformational change within numerous industries and businesses. Many economic experts have recognised the potential for data-driven innovations to contribute to broader societal transformation. For example, Manyika *et al.* (2013) have argued that the combination of large data sets and increasing amounts of open data are resulting in opportunities for 'data-driven innovations' as well as citizen empowerment and scientific learning (*Ibid.*, p. 4). Their description specifically – although perhaps unintentionally – indicates the ways in which these data innovations might also contribute to the creation of a knowledge society.

Policymakers have also recognised the potential centrality of data-driven innovations using open data and big data to enable societal transformation. In Europe, policymakers have intertwined their agendas on big data, open data and open access, expecting these to foster significant innovations and competitive advantages. European policymakers have called data 'the new gold' (Kroes 2011) and 'the new oil' (Kroes 2013) because of its income-generating potential, expecting it to reveal 'untapped business and economic opportunities including a predicted €140 billion profit' (Nagy-Rothengass 2014). These business and economic opportunities are primarily in the area of new services and applications for commercial and non-commercial purposes (Information Society 2012). They will feature 'an ecosystem of different types of players,' and increase the availability and transfer of knowledge to society (European Commission 2014, p. 5). The Chairman of the UK Competition and Markets Authority, David Currie, observed the potential impact of this dynamic:

> The rapidly expanding online market or markets [...] increasingly touch all aspects of business. Making sure competition works effectively in these markets will be a major priority [...] the growing collection, processing and use of consumer transaction data for commercial ends [...] is proving an increasingly important source of competitive advantage (cited in EDPS 2014, p. 32).

In addition, UK Cabinet Office minister Francis Maude encouraged entrepreneurs to make use of open data in the innovation process, asserting that:

> Data is in fact the new capital of the 21st Century, a highly valuable resource that is creating jobs and building whole new commercial markets [...] It is easier for entrepreneurs and businesses to analyse raw data and both sell on insights gained and create new and innovative products (BusinessZone 2012).

In the US, the 2012 Big Data Research and Development Initiative is a $200 million programme that aims to improve the 'ability to extract knowledge and insights from large and complex collections of digital data' and to 'help solve some of the Nation's most pressing challenges' (Office of Science and Technology Policy 2012). In both of these contexts, big data is expected to make a significant contribution to commercial innovation, societal good and knowledge transfer to members of the public.

A complex innovation space

Attempts to enable these data-driven innovations are occurring within a complex innovation space. While large companies have been at the forefront of achieving innovation using large data sets as a commercial resource, there is also some evidence that both large and small companies have been able to innovate using open data resources (Kroes 2013, 2011). However, this innovation remains uneven, and there is little information about the extent to which this innovation has permeated medium-sized companies or the extent to which SME or start-up innovation is sustainable and/or scalable beyond the beginning stages.

Large or small private sector organisations share a reliance upon open and free access to external data sources if they are to create (or add to) their own big data stores. Some large ICT firms, such as Google, Yahoo!, Facebook and Amazon as well as other companies like Siemens and Statoil are privileged actors within this space, because they can make use of extraordinarily large internal data sources to feed innovation in their respective markets. The data-driven innovations achieved by the likes of large American ICT companies such as Google and Facebook have received much attention in the media because of their use of data from members of the public to build new products and services. Other companies like Siemens and Statoil are also undertaking similar data-driven innovations to make their businesses more efficient and to aid decision-making (Vega-Gorgojo *et al.* 2015). However, these innovations are less visible because they focus on internal data resources and business-to-business transaction data, rather than consumer data.

With respect to SMEs, policymakers in many countries and regions have expressed expectations that start-ups and SMEs should benefit from this potential for data-driven innovation. The EC's Communications on a data-driven economy and enabling better access to scientific information (European Commission 2014, 2012b) specify SMEs as key beneficiaries of these policy changes, stating that they will provide support for SMEs who have previously had difficulties accessing scientific information and will enable them to develop, access and integrate data technologies or services into their products (European Commission 2014). The Big Data Research and Development Initiative in the US also expects data-driven innovations to support scientific discovery and to educate future generations of scientists and engineers as well as generate economic growth (BDSSG 2014). They anticipate that economic growth will also centre around small enterprises, with 'start-ups' featuring prominently within these discussions. Information from the Open Data 500 lists (see below) supports this assertion, but also raises questions about the extent to which SMEs have been able to capitalise on this opportunity for innovation.

Information from the Open Data 500 project, led by New York University, offers some insights into three specific national contexts and suggests that SMEs represent a significant proportion of organisations taking advantage of opportunities resulting from the intersection of big data and open data (Open Data 500 2015). The Open Data 500 is a list of organisations in the US, Mexico, Australia and Korea that are currently using open data for business purposes. The lists are compiled through outreach activities, expert recommendations and research by the team, and are intended to provide a broad, inclusive view of the field of open data innovations, not a representative sample of such organisations. Within the list, organisations provide information about their company, including a brief description, their address, the year they were founded, number of employees and additional information about their business models. The data suggests that, while SMEs do appear to be capitalising on open data, start-ups currently feature less prominently. Table 1 shows how many companies were classified as SMEs and start-ups in the 2015 list:

Table 1   Open Data 500 list of companies[3]

Country	# Companies listed	% SME (less than 200 employees)*	% Start-up (existing for 5 years or less)
USA	528	66%	33%
Mexico	108	73%	23%
Australia	66	86%	27%
Korea	301	74%	47%

* The Open Data 500 list classifies any company with fewer than 200 employees as a small business, which is differs slightly from the EU definition that an SME has fewer than 250 employees or an annual turnover less than €43m.

3   Figures on the number of employees and year of foundation were not available for all organisations.

Furthermore, 49 per cent of the US businesses listed had less than 50 employees, and 48 per cent of Korean companies had ten employees or fewer. However, it is worth noting that some large, established companies from the US, Mexico and Australia – particularly from the US – such as All State Insurance, Google, Deloitte, Thompson Reuters and IBM also feature in the list, demonstrating that some large companies are also using open data to generate economic value or advance or enhance their service delivery. Thus, it is clear that companies of all sizes are using open data to develop new products and services. However, this is a complex innovation space because of the lack of comprehensive investigation about the relative success and sustainability of the innovations achieved across different types of companies.

There is a danger that large corporate players may have a significant advantage over small companies, whose innovations may be unsustainable when situated in competition with large players. For example, the most notable changes are in developing the infrastructure needed to accommodate the management of big data effectively (e.g. Hadoop and other software), along with the tools and algorithms required to perform the analytical work that transforms data into information. Large companies certainly have greater resources available to both build large data sets and develop the infrastructure necessary to make full use of that data.

Nonetheless, SMEs and start-ups are considered to be nimble in comparison to large organisations and a regular source of innovation. Many start-ups are responsible for bringing about changes to frameworks that enable the analysis of big data, and are validating its potential through the creation of new applications, new technologies, and new business models based upon big data sets. In addition, they are amplifying this impact via links to other data sets, including those that are becoming increasingly available through open data and open access initiatives. Furthermore, with the open data movement, many SMEs and start-ups are also gaining access to a massive and growing set of open, big data.

However, SMEs may find themselves at a distinct disadvantage during the earliest evolutionary phases of the data-driven innovation cycle. Certainly, SMEs are highly motivated to tap into open data sources but, as they compete with large private sector organisations with greater internal resources, including in the form of proprietary data, they might initially find themselves at a competitive disadvantage. Within the big data ecosystem, however, opportunity may emerge for SMEs later in the technology evolution cycle, after governments, academics and large commercial actors have made major investments. This is not to imply that original ideas exist in a linear plane: innovative start-ups may create disruptive technologies at any point in time, or new applications may ultimately lead to the creation of new commercial industries. Innovation is more likely to be viewed as being iterative, with the data derived from one innovation carrying potential for driving others.

The use of GoogleMaps provides a powerful example of this. The innovative provision of location-based data through this service/platform/ API was initially mainly of benefit to Google itself, since it collected data and solidified its position by providing map applications to consumers. The value to SMEs evolved later, when the data was linked with local business listings and consumer geolocation data to provide suggestions on where to eat, shop, and play, with algorithms determining which suggestions were likely to appeal to individual consumers (see Figure 1). Uber, which was established in 2009, also built much of its success upon GoogleMaps data, eventually growing into a global enterprise. In turn, Uber and other companies are using data from GoogleMaps and other map applications to compete with Google in developing autonomous vehicles (Camhi 2015; Miller 2014). Thus, the original data that GoogleMaps collected has been re-harvested, driving innovation through the value of that data, which has been enhanced with more advanced technologies, ultimately creating a revolutionary business model in an entirely separate industry.

Figure 1   Innovation ecosystem using big data

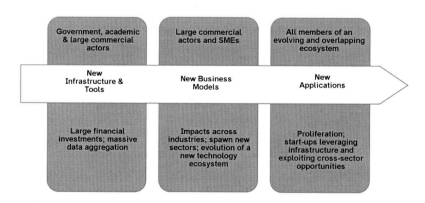

This example suggests that investment and infrastructure originating from large companies and other institutions may result in previously unforeseen opportunities and business models for smaller companies or start-ups. These opportunities emerge firstly within a bounded ecosystem and then permeate into a larger commercial and societal ecosystem. As such, rather than viewing data as 'the new oil', it may be more fitting to view data as akin to solar or wind power – a renewable energy source that will continue to provide cascading benefits through continual reuse, motivating the development of an infrastructure that delivers the energy itself, and setting the stage for the creation of myriad new applications. However, while this discussion demonstrates that policymakers are committed to supporting innovation in this space, some of the policies developed by, and advocated within, these circles may unintentionally create new obstacles against achieving such innovation.

Big data, open data and policy support

Governments in Europe, the US and other regions have been constructing policies intended to support the availability and opening of data for innovation and other public good. These are primarily focused on enabling innovation though opening access to data and, alongside policymakers, Chapter Four discusses the ways in which open data advocates have been playing a part in generating strategic support for such measures. However, other policy developments, which are meant to impact upon the use of data, create new challenges for combining data sets and extracting value from data assets, which can also affect the ability of stakeholders in this area to innovate.

In Europe, these policies have focused on access to government data and access to data which is created through publicly-funded research. With respect to government data in Europe, the 2013 Amended PSI Directive requires European member states to provide access to information held by the government, because such information 'constitute a vast, diverse and valuable pool of resources that can benefit the knowledge economy' (European Commission 2013b, p. 1). This Directive was amended from the original version, in response to the exponential increase in the amount of data available in the world and the 'continuous evolution in technologies for analysis, exploitation and processing of data', including 'the use, aggregation or combination of data' (*Ibid*.). Similarly, the Commission Decision 2011/833 requires that the EC must also provide access to documents and data held by the Commission, because these could be used to benefit citizens and companies who are seeking to provide new services (European Commission 2011). However, both documents state that government departments must respect intellectual property and personal privacy rights when providing open access to documents. This means that, in practice, data is often not subject to the directive.

Similarly, in the US, the 9 May 2013 Executive Order – 'Making Open and Machine Readable the New Default for Government Information' recognised the impact that data openness could have on promoting economic benefits (White House 2013). The US government asserted that, through providing open data to the public, 'entrepreneurs and innovators have continued to develop a vast range of useful new products and businesses using these public information resources' (*Ibid.*). Beyond providing greater access to data, governments are working to encourage use of this data through training programmes (GovLab Academy no date) and collaborative networks (Open Data Institute no date). Across all these regions, such releases of data must respect privacy and confidentiality, which can significantly reduce the amount of data that is made available. In the US, as in Europe, this provides important protections for those whose data might be contained within these data sets.

As well as legislating for open access, governments are also encouraging SMEs to use open data for innovation through financial incentives and other supports. The UK Digital Catapult programme has opened digital innovation centres in several locations, and has partnered with large industrial actors which will, in turn, connect with start-ups, SMEs and academics to work together to resolve areas of challenge in health and social care, the Internet of Things and data sharing (Preece 2015). Since the launch of the Open Government Partnership in 2011, 69 countries have developed, or are developing, national action plans that address issues of greater transparency and accountability (Data.gov.uk 2016).[4] In the UK, this includes making data more open, with over 22,000 data sets currently published online by the government (*Ibid.*).

On a broader scale, the quest for big-data-driven innovation is complemented (or perhaps complicated) by growing calls in the academic sector to develop research generated by universities into commercial patents or products. Since the 1990s, there has been increasing pressure to translate research directly into useful outcomes, supplementing the universities' role as institutions of knowledge production and knowledge transmission (D'Este and Patel 2007) to include technology transfer as well. This imperative is creating a quasi-commercial environment, as universities create and manage patent portfolios, often in contradiction to their affirmed commitment to generate open knowledge. In addition, universities may

4   As of 10 January 2016, 22,233 data sets had been published.

directly contribute to commercial innovation processes, investing private funds directly in companies and patents (Imperial Innovations 2012). One example of this is Imperial College, London's 'Imperial Innovations' fund, which has been investing in this way for 30 years, to fill the gap between scientific research and successful commercialisation in the UK.

Genome and stem cell research projects are further examples of research that has a strong commercial value for research groups and universities (Genome Canada 2014; Stem Cell Network 2009; Harmon *et al.* 2012). Governments are also recognising the potential benefits to the wider economy and, ultimately, taxpayers, by making publicly-funded data openly available to stimulate business innovation. For example, the UK government has provided funding for the relatively-recently launched Open Data Institute (ODI no date). However, such pushes towards open access sometimes undermine the sustainability of existing research infrastructure. For example, in the case of an open source software innovation, after initial funding has concluded, there is pressure to obtain ongoing funding for maintenance activities precisely at the time when investors are losing interest in the concept, because commercial competitors are expanding upon, and moving beyond, the original innovation. Ultimately, these market realities are discouraging some researchers in their quest to pursue such innovations.

In addition, policymakers, civil society organisations and academics have all been involved in supporting such policies, and advocates in this area champion definitions of open data that focus on providing access without any restrictions whatsoever, or restrictions which require continued openness. This has the inherent risk that, by promoting open data in this way, they are inadvertently making it difficult for those wishing to ensure some protection for the data produced as a result of commercial or research activities to justify such protections.

Open licensing frameworks are increasingly being used to open up data whilst maintaining some control over how the data is used. Creative Commons is the leading framework in this area, and their licences range from the CC0-licence (waiver), which does not reserve any rights, to licences that include restrictions against modification or commercial use, or require users to attribute the data to its original source or share any derived data under the same licence as the original data set (Creative Commons no date). Each of the licence elements included in the Creative Commons framework establishes some form of protection for those who originally created the data. Requirements to attribute the data build on, and protect, the reputation of those who originally created the data set. Protections against commercial use are partly intended to ensure that other profit-making organisations cannot compete with the originator, thus enabling the original creator themselves to innovate and retain their competitiveness. Protections against derivations may ensure that users do not combine the data with other, proprietary data sets to derive value that is inaccessible to the original creator. Such restrictions can prevent large internet companies from taking a start-up company's data and combining it with their own troves to offer services that the start-up would never be able to deliver on its own.

However, established definitions of open data make it difficult for stakeholders to conform to requirements to provide open access to data and concurrently realise commercial benefit from the data. As discussed in Chapter Three, many understandings of open data are based on the Open Knowledge Foundation (OKFN)'s definition, that:

> Open means anyone can freely access, use, modify, and share for any purpose (subject, at most, to requirements that preserve provenance and openness (OKFN 2015).

However, to ensure that data is open means that it must include technical and legal elements to achieve openness. For example, it must have an '(open) licence' that allows 'free access to and use of the data' by anyone, including commercial organisations (James 2013). In addition, there should be no technical barriers to using the data. The OKFN does, however, support licences that require attribution or oblige those using the data to share any data sets created as a result of their data (*Ibid.*), so it appears to support attribution and share-alike licences. Prominent open data organisations such as the Open Data Institute, Research Data Alliance and Confederation of Open Access repositories all use the OKFN definition of openness.

In addition, many governments also base their definition of open data on the OKFN's description. The US government's Open Data Policy Memorandum states that 'open data' is that which is publicly available, discoverable and usable by end users (OMB 2013). Open licences may be used, but there can be no restrictions on distributing, adapting or using the information for commercial or non-commercial purposes (*Ibid.*). This definition prohibits restrictions on commercial use, modification or distribution, since it refers to open government data, which is theoretically already owned by taxpayers. Nevertheless, it sets the standard of expectation for all open data. However, the US definition does consider the potential privacy impacts of releasing such data, recognising that this may impact on the extent to which data can be made open. In addition, the memorandum specifically states that, while the data itself may not contain personal information, those opening the data should consider a potential 'mosaic effect' of releasing disparate data which, when combined, might have privacy impacts for individuals and groups of people.

These definitions show that the most widely accepted international definitions of open data focus on making data as freely accessible and reusable as possible. However, these frameworks may have the effect of prioritising data openness rather than the potential to take advantage of the data to develop innovations, or the need to protect members of the public from unforeseen impacts of opening more and more data sets. For innovators, small businesses and new businesses, the need to protect information developed for innovation and commercial gains is a significant imperative if the knowledge society is going to reap the benefits of providing open data. Data licensing is one way that stakeholders can protect the intellectual property of some data sets and attempt to mitigate some of the potential negative impacts of open data and big data processing. It allows those who develop data sets to set conditions for the use of their data whilst also making it open. However, it is unclear whether policymakers and civil society organisations pushing for the benefits of open data are truly assisting innovations in these areas for SMEs and start-up companies as well as the public, who are supposed to gain the most. However, the US government's caution about a 'mosaic effect' of public data is an increasing threat to individuals, as governments, researchers and commercial organisations attempt to abide by the most restrictive definitions of open data, which may not adequately consider the impacts of big data. Therefore, policymakers need to consider the objectives of open data alongside economic goals, such as digital innovation, and social needs, including the protection of privacy and personal data.

The data development gap for European industry

Finally, there is some disparity in the development of innovative products and services that use both open data and big data in the commercial sector. It is clear that the US has been able to foster data-driven innovations much more successfully than Europe. Currently, Europe is characterised by marginal websites that do not harvest large amounts of personal data, and many European countries are reliant on services provided by external countries like the US, many of which are becoming as necessary for the economy as utilities such as transport or energy. Yet, although European policy is focused on addressing this development gap, it is worth considering whether other policy frameworks in Europe might contribute to a more responsible and attractive data sector for consumers.

The mobilisation of big data across Europe is being promoted by the Europe 2020 Strategy (European Commission 2010a), which was launched in March 2010. Part of this strategy is the Digital Agenda for Europe (DAE), which defines the role of technology as helping to 'maximise the social and economic potential of ICT,' in order to 'spur innovation, economic growth and improvements in daily life for citizens and businesses' through 'better health care, safer and more efficient transport solutions, a cleaner environment, new media opportunities and easier access to public services and cultural content' (European Commission 2010b, p. 3). In fact, the Commission acknowledges Europe's data development gap in comparison to the US, as the Communication on a data-driven economy demonstrates:

> there are fewer successful data companies in Europe than in the USA where large players have recognised the need to invest in tools, systems and new data-driven processes (European Commission 2014, p. 3).

However, until this point, Europe has been comparatively slow to adapt to the changes and opportunities posed by big data. With numerous US-based companies involved in the development and exploitation of technologies related to big data such as IBM, Google and Amazon,[5] large players and SMEs in Europe have been less visible in this space, although companies like Siemens, Philips and Statoil are implementing a number of data analytics programmes (Vega-Gorgojo et al. 2015).

Yet, at the same time, Europe has done particularly well in providing some protection for members of the public and data generators through other policy frameworks, such as the Data Protection Directive and the forthcoming General Data Protection Regulation as well as guidelines that protect intellectual property rights including those of database creators. In addition, Edward Snowden's 2013 information leaks about cross-border US government data surveillance practices[6] caused significant discomfort

---

5   US-EU Safe Harbor Principles had (until invalidated in October 2015) allowed enormous streams of data to be used by large commercial entities outside the EU. At the time of writing, it remains to be seen what the impact of the invalidation of Safe Harbor will have upon global commercial competition, as well as how its impact on other privacy legislation efforts.

6   See Lyon 2014 for a review of these practices and their implications. Lyon, David (2014) 'Surveillance, Snowden and Big Data: Capacities, consequences, critique', Big Data & Society, July–Dec 2014, 1–13.

for many European policymakers and citizens. The ensuing invalidation of the US-EU 'Safe Harbor' agreement means that many of these practices are no longer legally sound, so Europe has the opportunity to use its legislative framework to develop capacity that will protect the privacy and protection of personal data and intellectual property of its citizens.

Given that data – or access to and control of data – is the 'renewable energy' feeding the innovation engine, this opportunity creates a challenge for European actors to overcome, which extends beyond a typical market-based competitive advantage. Moreover, the absence of dominant corporations in the big data sector in Europe, and the dependency upon US systems, means that Europe needs to develop products and services that will retain the value of European data in Europe, rather than shifting that value to American companies. Ensuring that policy frameworks support the development of data-driven innovation in Europe, using data from people or other sources located within Europe, is an important imperative. In addition, Europe has a second opportunity to use the lessons from Snowden's security leaks to develop a big data sector that better protects privacy and intellectual property, and which ultimately leads to more responsible data innovations. Combined, this would contribute to a more transparent, trustworthy and responsible data economy that would ultimately feed into the creation of a knowledge society.

Conclusion

Promoting the provision of open data and ultimately combining those open data resources will eventually lead to the creation of data sets of significant volume and variety. As such, the evolution of open data will create big data sets that can further spur innovation and knowledge creation. However, this chapter has demonstrated that the use of big data has not resulted – and probably will not result in future – in a straightforward trajectory of innovation.

Instead, to date, it is unclear what types of organisations are realising the innovation benefits associated with big data and open data. Large American companies are emerging as clear innovators in this space, despite policy expectations that primarily SMEs and start-ups will benefit most from data-driven innovations. Large and relatively mature companies dominate media reports, academic research and collections of open data innovators, with the likes of Google, Amazon and IBM featuring prominently. While the Open Data 500 list shows that SMEs have benefitted from open data innovations, many of these businesses are start-ups with 10 employees or fewer, which may not be sustainable longer-term, particularly given the likelihood of them being bought up by larger competitors. In addition, while citizens are gaining some useful and attractive new products and services, many of these are predicated on the use of people's data in ways that may breach restrictive privacy frameworks in some countries and regions.

By discussing the data development gap between the US and Europe, this chapter has demonstrated that it is possible for countries or regions with a less developed data sector to learn from established data companies. Requirements for enhanced privacy or intellectual property protection could encourage improvements to be designed into data systems as they are being developed, rather than attempting to retrofit such protections into existing systems. This would encourage better participation in the data economy, which would enable data innovations to permeate more sectors of the economy. This could further contribute to the creation of a knowledge society, though the transparent and trustworthy use of data and more responsible data circulation to solve societal challenges and contribute to a more engaged and open relationship between citizens, commercial entities and governments.

10.   Conclusion

The idea of a knowledge society is still under-theorised and under-researched. Although there has been some debate on the subject within academic and policy circles, little theoretical and conceptual development has gone beyond the analysis of an information society. Debates on what comprises a knowledge society raise questions about how 'knowledge' is understood in contemporary society, how can it be shared and what values should underpin a knowledge society. The movement towards making data open in society is part of the wider debate about and how knowledge is shared at a society-wide level. The work of groups and movements that are championing open data reveal a set of underlying values beneath the drive for change, whilst simultaneously developing ecosystems and practices that will enable data to be made open. A principal question is whether the current activities and associated values pushing for change to implement open data are sufficient to support a transformation to a knowledge society.

To answer this question, there is a need to assess how far the open data movement is mobilising open data as part of a transformation to the knowledge society. Castelfranchi (2007) defines a knowledge society as one that generates, processes, shares and makes data available to everyone. He claims that a knowledge society has the capacity and capability to transform information into resources that can be used by society to take effective action. Furthermore, this action should be aligned with a progressive social agenda. However, as Stehr (1994) notes, there is a lack of understanding about how data can be shared democratically, or any process of debate and consensus for identifying what a progressive social agenda might be.

The development of the post-industrial and information society is characterised by the way that these types of society place knowledge at the centre of their economic and social relations. There is some opening up of knowledge to wider society in the Mode 2 framework of knowledge production, which embeds science and scientific institutions more closely within the social relations of contemporary society. However, repositioning of science and seeking to make its knowledge useful throughout wider society is, to some degree, based on market principles. Although contested, the notion of Mode 2 knowledge production sensitises analysis to some of the aspects of repositioning science in society. It highlights the development of market-type metrics to evaluate the value of knowledge, and it notes that knowledge is increasingly being evaluated by its impact on society.

The principles for guiding research and action are largely shaped by research funding bodies, scholarly societies, specific academic communities and institutions. These organisations may have socially-progressive values – for instance, social science funders might choose to support research into poverty alleviation. These funders' priorities are shaped by national and supra-regional governments, who design their research priorities in consultation with the academic community. Although there are democratic checks and balances, there is little overt debate about knowledge at the level of the general citizenry. Sweden is an exception, since it consults with the wider public about what research its government should be funding. In the competition to secure funding for their specific disciplines, every funding body therefore proposes agendas that can show impact and policy relevance, whilst also justifying some blue-skies and disinterested research.

Arguments for making data open are made within a similar framework, in relation to the value for money and return on investment that research will provide, particularly its potential benefit in broader social and economic contexts. The general policy impetus is based on the claim that much academic research is publicly-funded, so therefore the resultant data should be openly available to the wider public and stakeholders. The main value of data is seen to be its potential economic value, with some policy papers likening data to a commercial commodity, such as the 'new oil' (Kroes 2013). There is a belief (which has yet to be proven) that open data will support economic growth and add value to a range of industries, including the service and manufacturing sectors, and a range of different types of commercial actors, including large companies and SMEs. Beyond this, there is also recognition that open data may well contribute to broader societal goals such as creating a more inclusive society, and addressing a range of environmental concerns. This type of argument is based on a transactional model, where money is input into science and then science produces a set of outputs that can be applied in society. However, this approach overlooks the complexity of scientific development and knowledge development, both internally within disciplines and externally within the broader social relations of knowledge.

This, therefore, as considered in Chapter Two, raises some questions about the relationship between science and society, and the ways that science and society can be mutually accountable. Here, Fuller (1999) raises some fundamental points about open science and about science as a republic. He notes the complexities inherent in Castelfranchi's (2007) advocacy of a progressive social agenda, citing two main problems in considering how open data might be used by society. First, there is the issue of whose agenda is being followed. Society is diverse, with many demands and interests, so there would need to be an overarching body or set of principles to ensure that data is used in ways that are democratically legitimate to develop a progressive agenda that meets the needs of diverse groups. Second, intellectual property is based on the principle of universal availability, but it is shaped by market value concerns which result in ideas, data and concepts that are not too expensive being made open, whilst those that are too expensive remain closed. This means that the concept of 'public good' is understood in economic terms and shaped by what is affordable. These types of issues are in play in the social relationships of science and the relationship between science and society, so change is required at both institutional and research practice levels.

The rationale for developing open data is the imperative for wider and deeper interactions between science and society. The push for open data is positioned both within the institutions of science and government and outside them, in terms of civic society movements. As Chapter Six shows, perspectives on open data vary within scientific disciplines, so change towards open data varies in relation to these diverse research cultures and practices. In addition to cultural and ethical concerns, there is also a need to develop an infrastructure to support open data, and this is being discussed and developed through the idea of ecosystems of data and innovation. Here, we see the way in which institutions are seeking to ensure the production of sound and valid data as well as seeking to make data open. As Chapter Five shows, this is a complex process that will require significant investment. These are emerging in different ways, in response to the organisations involved, although as shown in Chapter Three, some general principles are developing, such as licensing and ensuring that data is machine-readable.

One area of knowledge production that demonstrates all of these factors and contradictions is the environmental sciences. Because these studies focus on wider concerns about, and changes in, the environment, they are driven by movements outside of the academy and supra-regional and national governments as well as scientists. As Chapter Seven shows, earth science, in particular, has made significant inroads in developing and using open data. In seeking to improve their use of data and to draw on a range of different data including big data, the earth science community has created a data ecosystem to support its work, the GEOSS, which was developed at both a technical and a governance level. This is because the scientists realised that they needed to have governance processes in place when they started to build a technical system for open data. Although its contributing communities support the principle of open data, they expressed an overarching concern about how the data would be used and the need for end-users to have appropriate tools to understand the data. This made the data-providers responsible for managing their own data and providing it in formats that enabled interoperability. The technical system and governance models relate to each other, because governance and data standards underpin and influence the technical aspects of the ecosystem. There are technical criteria that shape how the data can be deposited in particular institutional or disciplinary data ecosystems, such as GEOSS for the earth sciences, and shared, and these factors are influential in thinking through governance models. The ecosystem itself is made up of a range of data sources and communities, each with different legal and ethical frameworks and diverse types of data. Although the earth science community is paving the way for open data in technical and governance terms, the data is still mainly used by those working within the earth sciences field – whether as researchers or in other roles – so the impact of this data is somewhat limited.

Progress towards open access is varied and uneven in other areas of research, because each scientific discipline has its own internal dynamics, values and practices, which are shaping their attitudes to making data openly available. Data itself is constructed by the philosophical under-pinnings of each discipline, research focus, research design and process. Therefore, research practices are important in the creation, development and interpretation of data, and these are embedded within the conventions of different disciplines. Chapter Six shows how the frameworks and practices of specific disciplines shape the ways in which data can be made open, and to what level. Furthermore, the particularities of each research process means that attention needs to be paid to how such data can be made open. Although there are some general principles around making data open, these need to be interpreted and adapted to each specific case. This is requiring changes in research practice, as well as research culture, and this is being interpreted and implemented in various ways by different stakeholders.

However, it is not only research practice that has to change, Chapter Six also shows that there are some wider cultural issues involved as well. These include changes in the ways that researchers understand data ownership, and how they are rewarded for their efforts in data management and sharing. Currently academic researchers progress their careers in accordance with the amount of journal papers they publish and the amount of grant funding they obtain. Data is valuable in helping them to achieve this, because data underpins their publications and helps them build their reputation, which, in turn, enables grant capture. Because, to some degree, career development depends on 'owning' data, many researchers are understandably reluctant to share their data and make it open to others. This requires a change, to where data sets and their quality are also recognised in evaluating researchers' careers, along with a process by which data can be cited by others. There is some development in this area by, for example, services that issue permanent, digital object identifiers (DOIs) for data that allow the data to be cited like a publication.[1] These are alterations in the research environment that will require a change to the socialisation and training experiences of PhD students and early career researchers. It also means that established researchers and supervisors will have to adapt to the new environment, learning new practices and processes.

Embedded within research practices and sensibilities are concerns about the ethical aspects of research and regulatory frameworks around data sharing. When addressing these issues it becomes apparent that data has distinctive properties, even when it is viewed as a commodity, and these properties raise special ethical issues. For example, one of the most pressing issues concerns data which is gathered from human beings, whether for medical or social science research. There are robust regulations in place to protect human subjects in research, including ensuring their anonymity and confidentiality. Most of the data is already anonymous but extra ethical processes are needed to ensure informed consent for the data to be reused. Yet, each disciplinary area has to navigate its own ethical, legal and regulatory frameworks; however, some general solutions to issues have already been found. For example, licensing can be used to provide limitations and requirements around the reuse of data. Other processes include editorial review, which uses existing disciplinary and institutional frameworks to make sure that data is made open ethically and legally. Chapter Eight extends the ethical issues of research into wider social and commercial area of data use, especially regarding the challenges of addressing privacy, data protection and IP issues of open data. These processes are still developing and, given the newness of the context, legal and ethical bodies are currently seeking to understand the context more clearly. Thus, at the moment, open data advocates are devising community-driven solutions to making data open whilst addressing legal and ethical concerns.

---

1   A DOI is a serial code used to identify unique objects and is used for electronic documents such as journal articles. For example, figshare is an online digital repository where researchers can preserve and share their research outputs, including figures, datasets, images, and videos. It is free to upload content and free to access, in adherence to the principle of open data.

Another feature in the data landscape is the emergence of big data. This is often a by-product of a series of digital platforms and systems which collect large amounts of data, and developments around open data will exponentially increase the amount of data available. While the availability of this data is expected to result in substantial innovations in research, commercial practice and government processes, the innovation process will probably not be straightforward. Data owned by large, commercial organisations is likely to remain proprietary, while other actors will be basing their innovations on open data sets, which large commercial players may also access. Thus, as shown in Chapter Nine, some small organisations, SMEs and groups may find themselves at a disadvantage within this ecosystem. Nevertheless, innovations by these large actors will eventually implicate other actors within the larger ecosystem, since innovations permeate the commercial and social fabric. Attempts to protect some data sets in order to support innovation by small actors and protect personal privacy may affect the extent to which such advances can be achieved. However, these protections should be viewed as opportunities for further innovation, particularly chances to create a responsible, privacy-friendly and trustworthy data-driven innovation space. Such a space will contribute to the emergence of a knowledge society through increased public trust in, and use of, data on a more widespread basis.

There are ongoing developments in making research data open, which differ from privately-owned big data. To assess and understand the current phase of this process, there is a need to consider how open data features in open science. The practice of research varies across academic and scientific disciplines. As shown in Chapter Six, each discipline or field of disciplines has its own culture that shapes the way that data is produced, interpreted and shared. Although research policy is changing research culture, as shown by the current focus on demonstrating the impact of research, other factors affect the realities of making research data openly available. These include the need for specialised technology to access certain types of raw data and subject-specific expertise required to interpret the data. These issues need further consideration in order to fully understand how open science relates to wider society and societal stakeholders.

Knowledge is growing in other areas, such as in open government, where governments have been active in creating access to public data and are beginning to understand how open data can be made available. However, as shown in Chapter Four, citizens' ability and preference to use open data needs to increase if open data is to make a significant contribution to social transparency and innovation. The work of open data civil society groups has also shown that there is lack of knowledge around preparing open data for use. These groups are early leaders in the field and, as discussed in Chapter Three, they have developed an understanding of what is needed in terms of technology, governance, research practices and ethical and legal frameworks to facilitate making data openly available and meaningful to users. There is still work to do in each of these areas, some of which are more developed than others; however, there are now some building blocks in place to facilitate open data.

Nonetheless, progress is uneven. Although, as Chapter Seven shows, the earth science community has made significant advances around open data governance and technology, whereas progress in research practice is variable, with some disciplines adapting to open data more easily than others. Some political issues are also acting as barriers to mainstreaming open data, for example the federal political system in the US that has slowed developments there. The mobilisation of open access to data is therefore uneven across subject areas and nations, resulting in fragmentation across the open data landscape. On one level, this is not surprising, because the way that data is produced, managed and curated varies in relation to its research area. On another level, if the vision is one of a knowledge society in which data supports social action – and this vision is usually based on normative ideas of progressive action – then there needs to be a consistency in and across ecosystems – as well as support for fostering interpretive communities. To summarise, open data activists and policymakers have created a situation where there is awareness about open data and where researchers across sectors and disciplines are feeling the impetus to make their data open.

Chapter Four shows that a range of open data advocates have begun mobilising open data in diverse ways. Many of these are following the values established by the early developers of the internet and WWW – values of freedom and openness, which are interpreted in terms of open source, open hardware and open content. Although this interpretation of openness has been made tangible through concrete ways of developing technology and sharing content, it reflects an underlying philosophical principle that is wider than a technological world. This vision is based on 'universalist' principles, which seek to create an environment that enables people to participate in discussions on a wide range of issues in an open way. Berners-Lee (1999) sees this as essential for realising the freedom to send content anywhere across a network, accompanied by a freedom of association to foster a society in which the needs of the collective are balanced with the needs of the individual. This social vision is seen in the work of open data advocates, who focus on different areas of open data that contribute to the end result of facilitating a more open society in some way. They do not necessarily theorise about what this society might entail and, in some ways, they assume that just having data open will enable societal actors to develop and shape the society. However, this raises questions about how far open data advocates can go beyond enabling open data to mobilise a knowledge society.

To answer this question it is important to examine who the open data advocates are and how they relate to each other in mobilising action. The key actors are civil society organisations, national governments and supra-national bodies. Civil society networks including ODI, are very active in lobbying for open data. Other civil society networks, such as the OKFN, are supporting the development of key open data enablers, such as licensing criteria and widening understanding of how to work with data through training and education. The G8, OECD and national governments have pushed, and continue to push, a range of open data policy directives within their legislative frameworks. The combination of these actors has been instrumental in the development of open data, and continues to exert influence – but can this be classed as a social movement? If so, what are its characteristics?

Social movements refer to types of collective action which are wide-ranging, diverse and characterised in various ways. Melucci (1996) argues that it is important to explore the formation and maintenance of the cognitive frameworks and the social relationships that form the basis of collective action. In late modernity, this action interacts at cultural and structural levels – and these often combine or interact with each other. As discussed in Chapter Four, one of the characteristics of open data advocates' activity is the affinitive relationship between civil society activists and formal governmental advocates and policymakers. Most social movements are primarily located within civil society and operate with a lifeworld focus in creating a normative consensus to instigate change across governmental, structural and political arenas as well as at cultural, economic and social levels. They therefore instigate purposive collective action to transform values and institutions. In contrast, governments have subscribed to the visions put forward by the open data movement, and joined their call to develop open data.

The process of open data mobilisation was rooted in civil society. As already mentioned, this was built by people working within a framework of openness that was based on the early internet developers. There was, and continues to be, individual networks that seek to push the value of openness in terms of open data, and seek to foster change at an institutional level by developing the processes and ecosystems that will enable open data. These networks exist as individual entities but they link at certain points, which give them additional power from being a network of networks (Castells 2009). These networks and networks of networks are instrumental in driving forward the idea of open data and providing a vision of its benefits to society – and, as such, they have formed a loose social movement. As a loose social movement, it has also developed instruments to facilitate open data, such as licensing and training. Advocates from civil society have also lobbied governments and actors such as the OECD to support open data though policy drives.

From the perspective of formal bodies such as governments, open data is also a constituent in broader imperatives, like open government and open innovation. These have the potential to help them counter a public trust deficit by facilitating a more transparent, responsive and open government as well as addressing the issue of economic growth and innovation in an information society. This, together with a shared imagination of the possibilities of open data, means that the civil agenda is being developed through policy. This shows how a civil society network of networks has been joined by policymakers at national, world regional and global levels. This would seem to signify a social movement that is advocating and developing open data, and which has a shared vision of the benefits of open data. Each organisation may emphasise one aspect of that vision over another – some stressing social benefits and others economic benefits – but there is an overarching belief of the value of open data. The combined efforts of advocates, networks and institutions have generated a distinctive type of social movement characterised as a network of networks, with affiliations between civil society action and policy actors and action.

As discussed in Chapters Three and Four, this type of movement is a major actor in fostering new ideas about how data could be used in society, whilst also focusing on some of the main actions and processes required to achieve this. The open data movement focuses on key enablers that have been discussed in the book, such as the socio-technical changes required, licensing, legal and ethical issues, and ways of monitoring open data readiness at a global level. There are, however, some substantial barriers and risks to making certain data openly available. One is the way in which scientific data is managed, since the scientific methods involve lengthy and costly verification processes that may well hamper efforts to make its data openly available. Another is the value of big data, which is currently largely held by big commercial companies that lack any incentive to make such data openly available. Furthermore, the uneven development of open data readiness means that open data may, in fact, end up reproducing and increasing inequalities at the global level. However, in certain national, disciplinary or institutional cases there is a strong policy push to make this data more openly available, which may open its access and support its use by a wider range of actors, including those in civic society.

The open data movement is also supporting a range of educational programmes that will enhance data skills across societies, a key factor if access to data will provide data that is meaningful and useful to a range of societal actors. The open data movement is monitoring inequalities in this area and is seeking to support less-developed countries and regions. The open data movement is, therefore, a significant actor in making data openly available and ensuring that this access is meaningful and useful.

Nonetheless, the development of a new data ecosystem is only in its infancy. While RECODE examined issues like governance, interoperability, data curation, licensing and ethical issues, these need significant further examination both beyond open access to research data and as the open data ecosystem develops. Furthermore, institutions and organisations in both the public and the private sectors are reconsidering how they value data and how they might share and make that data open in ways that could benefit society. However, there are three significant gaps in the work of this broadly-defined movement: (1) a lack of theorisation or vision about how open data features in a transformation to a knowledge society; (2) where science should be positioned within an open data society; and (3) the need to develop interpretive communities. If these points are not resolved, then the open data movement may continue to contribute towards a transformation to knowledge society, but will not sufficient to mobilise a knowledge society.

There therefore needs to be further consideration about what types of societal change is required to transform an information society into a knowledge society. In particular, this means addressing the details of Castelfranchi's (2007) point that a knowledge society involves using data in ways that allow society to take effective action. Here, attention must be paid to the distinction between a knowledge society and a science society. In terms of Mode 2 knowledge production, science is being pushed into an ever-closer relationship with social and economic actors, as well as becoming more centrally located within social relations. However, this is not sufficient to support a transformation to a knowledge society.

One factor in all these issues is how the substance – data – might be used in society, for what purpose and by whom. Here, questions of power are important, since open access to data could potentially bring about an open society but, if exploited by a few with the skills and networks to use it, then new forms of domination may emerge. Furthermore, in terms of the social role of science, it is important to consider whether knowledge derived from data may create risks by an inexperienced interpretation of the data that could result in making societies more fragile. The use of data in developing knowledge can generate a capacity for action, but that action can be for a variety of purposes. Therefore, a transformation to a knowledge society requires changes in education and in cultural frameworks to ensure that any knowledge society developed is progressively humane and humanistic.

In conclusion, therefore, although the open data movement is an important actor in fostering open data, there will have to be a shift in social imagination about how to use data, as Stehr (1994) argues, aligned with further development of a data ecosystem to mobilise a knowledge society. Nonetheless, the open data movement has moved society some way towards being able to mobilise and transform it into a knowledge society.

Bibliography

Adams, Caralee (no date) 'Open Access in Latin America: Embraced as Key to the Visibility of Research Outputs', SPARC. http://www.sparc.arl.org/news/open-access-latin-america-embraced-key-visibility-research-outputs.

Amedeo, A. and Baumann, I. (2013) *Applicability of WTO law to the Copernicus Data and Information Policy*, (Specific Contract No GMES/G.4/2013/Lot3- SI2.646761 implementing Framework Service Contract 89/PP/ENT/2011- LOT3(GMES/H4/201KÌ3), (Köln, Germany: BHO Legal).

APARSEN (2012) 'Report on Peer Review of Research Data in Scholarly Communication', 30 April.

Australian Government (2015) 'Open data toolkit' https://toolkit.data.gov.au/index.php?title=Policy.

Beagrie, Neil, Lavoie, Brian and Woollard, Matthew (2010) *Keeping Data Safe (Phase 2)*, (London: JISC).

Beagrie, Neil (no date) 'Keeping Research Data Safe Factsheet' http://www.beagrie.com/static/resource/KRDS_Factsheet_0711.pdf.

Becker, C. (1992) *Living and Relating: An Introduction to Phenomenology* (London: Sage).

Bell, D. (1973) *The Coming of the Post-Industrial Society* (New York: Basic Books).

Berger, P.L. and Luckmann, T. (1967) *The Social Construction of Reality* (London: The Penguin Press).

Berners-Lee, T. (1999) *Weaving the Web: The Past, Present and Future of the World Wide Web by its Inventor* (San Francisco, CA: Harper Collins).

Berners-Lee, T. (2012) 'Open Up! World Wide Web Foundation' http://webfoundation.org/2012/11/tech-innovation-and-open-government-convene-at-open-up-2012-nov-13-in-london/.

Berry, D. M. (2008), *Copy, Rip Burn: The Politics of Copyleft and Open Source* (London: Pluto Press).

Beynon-Davies P. (2002) *Information Systems: An Introduction to Informatics in Organisations* (Basingstoke: Palgrave).

Bloom, T. (2013) 'Data Access for the Open Access Literature: PLOS's Data Policy', Public Library of Science, 12 December. http://www.plos.org/data-access-for-the-open-access-literature-ploss-data-policy/.

Borgman, C.L. (2012) 'The Conundrum of Sharing Research Data', *Journal of the American Society for Information Science and Technology*, 63:6. http://dx.doi.org/10.2139/ssrn.1869155.

Bossi S. and Poggi, M. (1994) *Romanticism in Science: Science in Europe, 1790–1840 (Boston Studies in the Philosophy and History of Science.* Dordrecht/Boston/London, Kluwer Academic Publishers.

Boyd, D. and Crawford, K. (2012) 'Critical Questions for Big Data', *Information, Communication & Society*, 15:5, 662–679.

Brin, S. (1998) *Extracting Patterns and Relations from the World Wide Web* http://ilpubs.stanford.edu:8090/421/1/1999-65.pdf.

Brin, D. (1999) *The Transparent Society: Will Technology Force us to Choose between Privacy and Freedom?* (New York: Basic Books).

Brown, M. and White, W. (2013) 'University of Southampton: A Partnership Approach to Research Data Management', in: Pryor, *et al.* (2013) *Delivering Research Data Management Services: Fundamentals of Good Practice* (London: Facet Publishing).

BusinessZone (2012) 'Minister tells SMEs: Tap into Our Data to Innovate Globally as UK Entrepreneurs'. http://www.businesszone.co.uk/delete/politics/minister-tells-smes-tap-into-our-data-to-innovate-globally-as-uk-entrepreneurs.

Camhi, Jonathan (2015) 'Why Uber is Pouring Money into Developing Autonomous Cars', *Business Insider.* http://www.businessinsider.com/why-uber-is-investing-in-autonomous-cars-2015-8.

Campbell, John, L., Rustad, Lindsey E., Porter, John H., Taylor, Jeffrey, R., Dereszynski, Ethan W., Shanley, James B., Gries, Corinna *et al.* (2013) 'Quantity is Nothing Without Quality: Automated QA/QC for Streaming Environmental Sensor Data', *BioScience*, 63:7, 574–585.

Carlson, S. and Anderson, B. (2007) 'What Are Data? The Many Kinds of Data and Their Implications for Data Re-Use', *Journal of Computer-Mediated Communication*, 12: 2.

Castelfranchi, C. (2007) 'Comment. Six Critical Remarks on Science and the Construction of the Knowledge Society', *Journal of Science Communication*, SISSA – International School for Advanced Studies, 1–3.

Castells, M. (1996) *The Rise of the Network Society* (Oxford: Blackwell).

Castells, M. (2001) *The Internet Galaxy: Reflections on the Internet, Business and Society* (Oxford: Oxford University Press).

Castells, M. (2009) *Communication Power* (Oxford: Oxford University Press).

Cohen, R., and Rai, S. (2000) *Global Social Movements* (London: Athlone Press).

Copernicus (2016) 'Copernicus, the European EO Programme'. www.copernicus.eu/.

Cornford, J., Wilson, R., Baines, S., and Richardson, R. (2015) 'Local Governance in the New Information Ecology: The Challenge of Building Interpretative Communities', *Public Money and Management* 33, 201–208.

Cox, A. M. and Pinfield, S. (2013) 'Research Data Management and Libraries: Current Activities and Future Priorities', *Journal of Librarianship and Information Science*, [preprint].

Creamer, A. T., Morales, M.E., Kafel, D., Crespo, J., Martin, E.R. (2012) 'A Sample of Research Data Curation and Management Courses', *Journal of eScience Librarianship*, 1:2, article 4.

Creative Commons (no date) 'About CC0 – 'No rights reserved'. http://creativecommons.org/about/cc0.

Creative Commons (2015) 'About the Licenses' http://creativecommons.org/licenses/.

Cunningham, A. and Jardine, N. (1990) *Romanticism and the Sciences* (Cambridge: Cambridge University Press).

D'Este, P. and Patel, P. (2007) 'University-Industry Linkages in the UK: What are the Factors Underlying the Variety of Interactions with Industry?', *Research Policy*, 36, 1295–1313.

Dallmeier-Tiessen, Sunje, Darby, Robert, Gitmans, Kathrin, Lambert, Simon, Suhonen, Jari and Wilson, Michael (2012) *Compilation of Results on Drivers and Barriers and New Opportunities*, http://www.alliancepermanentaccess.org/index.php/community/current-projects/ode/outputs/.

Data Archiving and Networked Services (DANS) (2016) 'Easy'. https://easy.dans.knaw.nl/ui/home.

Data Archiving and Networking Service (no date) 'Data Archiving and Networking Service|Homepage', http://www.dans.knaw.nl.

Dataverse Network project, The (no date) 'History', http://thedata.org/book/history

Data.Gov.UK (2016) 'Data', https://data.gov.uk/data/search.

Davies, T. (2013) *Open Data Barometer 2013 Global Report*, http://www.opendataresearch.org/barometer.

Davies, T. and Bawa, Z. (2012) 'The Promises and Perils of Open Government Data (OGD)', *The Journal of Community Informatics*, North America, 8, April Available at: http://ci-journal.net/index.php/ciej/article/view/929. Date accessed: 15 February 2016.

De Vries, Marc (2012) *Open Data and Liability*, European Public Sector Information Platform Topic Report No. 2012 / 13.

Dersin, Pierre (2015) 'Systems of systems', *IEEE Reliability Society*. http://rs.ieee.org/component/content/article/9/77-system-of-systems.html.

Desnos, Yves-Louis (2003) 'The GMES/Copernicus Sentinels Missions and their Exploitation for Science and Applications' European Space Agency.

Digital Curation Centre (2012) Curation Policies and Support Services of the Main UK Research Funders, http://www.dcc.ac.uk/sites/default/files/documents/RC%20policy%20 overview%20v2.2.pdf.

Dillenberger, J. (1960) Protestant Thought and Natural Science: A Historical Interpretation (Doubleday Publishers: New York City).

Dillo, Ingrid, Horik, Rene van and Scharnhorst, Andrea (2013) 'Training in Data Curation as Service in a Federated Data Infrastructure – the FrontOffice/BackOffice Model', http:// arxiv.org/pdf/1309.2788.pdf.

Di Pippo, Simonetta (2014) UNOOSA's Commitment to Earth Observations, Apogeo. http:// apogeospatial.com/unoosas/.

Donovan, Anna, Finn, Rachel and Wadhwa, Kush (2014) Report on Public Perceptions and Social Impacts Relevant to Big Data, BYTE D2.2.

Drucker, P. (1969) The Age of Discontinuity. Guidelines to our Changing Society (New York: Harper & Row).

Dryad (2013) 'Business Plan and Sustainability' http://wiki.datadryad.org/Business_Plan_and _Sustainability.

Economist (2014) Every Click you make. Tracking the Tracker, 11 September. http://www.economist.com/blogs/newsbook/2014/09/digital-advertising-tracking-trackers.

Edwards, Paul N., Mayerik, Matthew S, Batcheller, Archer L., Bowker Geoffrey C., and Borgman, Christine L. (2011) 'Science Friction: Data, Metadata, and Collaboration', Social Studies of Science, 41:5, 667–690.

Elster, J. (1993) Political Philosophy (Cambridge: Cambridge University Press).

EMA/9sight (2013) Operationalizing the Buzz: Big Data, http://www.enterprisemanagement. com/research/asset.php/2641/Operationalizing-the-Buzz:-Big-Data-2013.

European Commission (2003a) Directive 2003/98/EC of The European Parliament and of The Council of 17 November 2003 on the Reuse of Public Sector Information, OJ L 345, 90–96.

European Commission (2003b) Directive 2003/4/EC of The European Parliament and of The Council of 28 January 2003 on Public Access to Environmental Information and Repealing Council Directive 90/313/EEC, OJ L 41, 26–32.

European Commission (2010a) Marine Knowledge 2020: Marine Data and Observation for Smart and Sustainable Growth, COM (2010) 461 final, Brussels.

European Commission (2010b) Commission Regulation (EU) No 268/2010 of 29 March 2010 Implementing Directive 2007/2/EC of the European Parliament and of the Council as Regards the Access to Spatial Data Sets and Services of the Member States by Community Institutions and Bodies under Harmonised Conditions, OJ L 83.

European Commission (2010c) Europe 2020: A Strategy for Smart, Sustainable and Inclusive Growth, COM (2010) 2020, Brussels.

European Commission (2010d) A Digital Agenda for Europe, COM (2010) 245 final/2, Brussels.

European Commission (2011) Commission Decision of 12 December 2011 on the Reuse of Commission Documents, 2011/833/EU, Brussels.

European Commission (2012a) Towards Better Access to Scientific Information: Boosting the Benefits of Public Investments in Research, COM (2012) 401 final.

European Commission (2012b) Commission Recommendation on Access to and Preservation of Scientific Information, COM (2012) 4890 final, Brussels. http://ec.europa.eu/ research/science-society/document_library/pdf_06/recommendation-access-and -preservation-scientific-information_en.pdf.

European Commission (2013a) Guidance on the Regulation of Access to Spatial Data Sets and Services of the Member States by Community Institutions and Bodies under Harmonised Conditions.

European Commission (2013b) Directive 2013/37/EU Amending Directive 2003/98/EC on the Reuse of Public Sector Information, *OJ*, L175, pp. 1–8.

European Commission (2014) Towards a Thriving Data-driven Economy, COM (2014) 442 final, Brussels.

European Commission (2015) 'European Legislation on Reuse of Public Sector Information'. https://ec.europa.eu/digital-agenda/en/legislative-measures.

European Commission (2016a) 'Europe 2020 Strategy'. http://ec.europa.eu/digital-agenda/digital-agenda-europe.

European Commission (2016b) 'Europe 2020'. http://ec.europa.eu/europe2020/index_en.htm.

European Commission (2016c) 'Open Data'. https://ec.europa.eu/digital-agenda/en/open-data-0.

European Commission (2016d) *Guidelines on Open Access to Scientific Publications and Research Data in Horizon 2020*, Version 2.1. http://ec.europa.eu/research/participants/data/ref/h2020/grants_manual/hi/oa_pilot/h2020-hi-oa-pilot-guide_en.pdf.

European Data Protection Supervisor A (2014) *Privacy and Competitiveness in the Age of Big Data*, Brussels, https://secure.edps.europa.eu/EDPSWEB/webdav/shared/Documents/Consultation/Opinions/2014/14-03-26_competitition_law_big_data_EN.pdf.

European Parliament and the Council (2007) Directive 2007/2/EC of 14 March 2007 Establishing an Infrastructure for Spatial Information in the European Community (INSPIRE), *OJ* L 108, 25 March 2007.

European Parliament and the Council (2010) Regulation (EU) No 911/2010 of the European Parliament and of the Council of 22 September 2010 on the European Earth Monitoring Programme (GMES) and its initial operations (2011 to 2013), *OJ* L 276.

European Space Agency –Earth Observation Programme Board (2009) The Joint Principles for a Sentinel Data Policy, ESA/PB-EO (2009) 98, rev. 1, Paris, 23 October.

European Space Agency (2012) 'Sentinel Data Policy and Access to Data', *Workshop on GMES Data and Information Policy*, Brussels, 12–13 January.

Eurostat Big Data Task Force (2014) Towards a Thriving Data-driven Economy – Communication of the European Commission COM (2014) 422 final.

Finn, Rachel, Wadhwa, Kush, Taylor, Mark, Sveinsdottir, Thordis, Noorman, Merel, Wyatt, Sally and Sondervan, Jeroen (2014) *Legal and Ethical Issues in Open Access to Research Data*, RECODE D3.1.

Finn, Rachel L., Watson, Hayley and Wadhwa, Kush (2015) 'Exploring Big 'Crisis' Data in Action: Potential Positive and Negative Externalities', *Proceedings of the 12th International ISCRAM Conference*, Kristiansand, Norway.

Fish, S. (1980) *Is There a Text in This Class.* (Cambridge, MA: Harvard University Press).

Freeman, C. (1992) 'Technology, Progress and the Quality of Life', in: Freeman, C. (1992) *The Economics of Hope: Essays on Technical Change, Economic Growth and the Environment* (London: Pinter), 212–230.

Freeman, C. (1994) 'The Economics of Technical Change, Critical Survey', *Cambridge Journal of Economics* 18, 463–514.

Freimna, Lesley, Ward, Catharine, Jones, Sarah, Molloy, Laura, Snow, Kellie, (2010) *Incremental Scoping study and Implementation plan: A Pilot Project for Supporting Research Data Management*, University of Cambridge, University of Glasgow.

Fry, J., Lockyer, S., Oppenheim, C., Houghton, J. and Rasmussen, B. (2008) *Identifying Benefits Arising from the Curation and Open Sharing of Research Data Produced by UK Higher Education and Research Institutes.* Loughborough University: Centre for Strategic Economic Studies.

Fuller, S. (2002) [1988]. *Social Epistemology* (2nd ed.). (Bloomington, IN: Indiana University Press).

Fuller, S. (1993) [1989]. *Philosophy of Science and its Discontents* (2nd edition) (New York: Guilford Press).

Fuller, S. (1997) *Science. Concepts in Social Sciences* (Milton Keynes, UK/Minneapolis, MN: Open University Press/University of Minnesota Press).

Fuller, S. (1999) *The Governance of Science: Ideology and the Future of the Open Society. Issues in Society.* (Buckingham, UK/Philadelphia, PA: Open University Press).

Fuller, S. (2006) *The Philosophy of Science and Technology Studies.* (New York: Routledge).

Gabridge, Tracy (2009) *The Last Mile: Liaison Roles in Curating Science and Engineering Research Data, Research Library Issues, A Bimonthly Report from ARL CNL and SPARC*, August. http://old.arl.org/bm~doc/rli-265-gabridge.pdf.

Gartner (2014) 'Gartner's 2014 Hype Cycle for Emerging Technologies Maps the Journey to Digital Business'. http://www.gartner.com/newsroom/id/2819918.

Gartner (2015) 'Gartner's 2015 Hype Cycle for Emerging Technologies Identifies the Computing Innovations That Organizations Should Monitor'. http://www.gartner.com/newsroom/id/3114217.

Genome Canada (2014) 'Entrepreneurship Education in Genomics (EEG) Program'. http://www.genomecanada.ca/.

Gibbons, M., Limoges, C., Nowotny, H., Schwartzman, S., Scott, P. and Trow, P (1994) *The New Production of Knowledge: The Dynamics of Science and Research in Contemporary Societies* (London: Sage).

Goddard, J.B. (1992) 'New Technology and the Geography of the UK Information Economy', in: Robins, K. *Networks of Transactions,* Times Higher Education Supplement.

Gorgolewski, Krzysztof J., Margulies, Daniel S. and Milham, Michael P. (2014) 'Making Data Sharing Count: A Publication-Based Solution', *Frontiers in Neuroscience*, 7:9. http://www.ncbi.nlm.nih.gov/pmc/articles/PMC3565154/.

GovLab Academy (no date) 'About Us'. http://govlabacademy.org/about.html#about-govlab.

Group on Earth Observations (GEO) (no date) 'GEO – Group on Earth Observations'. http://earthobservations.org/index.shtml.

Group on Earth Observations (2005) *10-Year Implementation Plan Reference Document* (Noord-wijk, NL: ESA Publications Division).

Group on Earth Observations (2010) *GEOSS Data Sharing Action Plan*, GEO-VII Plenary document, Beijing, China, 3–4 November.

Group on Earth Observations (2014) 'GEO Appathon'. http://geoappathon.org/.

Group on Earth Observations (2014b) 'Group on Earth Observations'. www.earthobservations.org.

Habermas, J. (1984) *The Theory of Communicative Action: Reason and Rationalization of Society* (Boston, MA: Beacon).

Habermas, J. (1987) *The Structural Transformation of the Public Sphere: An Inquiry into the Category of Bourgeois Society* (Cambridge, MA: MIT Press).

Halbert, Martin (2013) *Prospects for Research Data Management* (Washington, D.C.: UNT Digital Library). http://digital.library.unt.edu/ark:/67531/metadc234912/.

Harmon, S.H.E., Caulfield, T. and Joly, Y. (2012a) 'Commercialization Versus Open Science: Making Sense of the Message(s) in the Bottle', *Medical Law International*, 12:1, 3–10.

Harmon, S.H.E., Caulfield, T. and Joly, Y. (2012b) 'Open Science Versus Commercialization: A Modern Research Conflict? *Genome Medicine*, 4:17.

Harrison, C. Pardo, T.A. and Cook, M. (2012) 'Creating Open Government Ecosystems: A Research and Development Agenda' *Future Internet* 4, 900–928.

Henttu, Heikki, Izaret, Jean-Manuel and Potere, David (2012) *Geospatial Services: A $1.6 Trillion Growth Engine for the US Economy*, BCG perspectives. https://www.bcg.com/documents/file109372.pdf.

High Level Expert Group (2010) *Riding the Wave: How Europe can Gain from the Rising Tide of Scientific Data*. Final report of the High Level

Expert Group on Scientific Data. http://ec.europa.eu/information_society/newsroom/cf/document.cfm?action=display&doc_id=707.

Hivan, J. and Titah, R. (2015) *Citizen Participation in Open Data Use at the Municipal Level* (Montreal: Unpublished research report).

Holzner, B. Dunn, W. N. Shahidullah, M. (1987) 'An Accounting Scheme for Designing Science Impact Indicators The Knowledge System Perspective', *Science Communication* 9(2):173–204.

Houghton, J. (2014) 'Impacts of Increased Access and New Modes of Consumption', *Proceedings for Workshop on Assessing the Socio-economic Impacts and Value of 'Open' Geospatial Information:* 28–29 October 2014, George Washington University, Washington D.C., Eliot School of International Affairs.

Hughes, J.A. (1990) *The Philosophy of Social Research* (London: Longman).

Information Society (2012) 'Big Data at Your Service', *Europa*. http://ec.europa.eu/information_society/newsroom/cf/dae/itemdetail.cfm?item_id=8337.

Infrastructure for Spatial Information in Europe (INSPIRE) (2013) 'Good Practice in Data and Service Sharing'. http://inspire.ec.europa.eu/documents/

Data_and_Service_Sharing/GoodPractice_%20DataServiceSharing_v3.pdf.

James, Laura (2013) 'Defining Open Data', *Open Knowledge Blog*, 3 Oct. http://blog.okfn.org/2013/10/03/defining-open-data/#sthash.rEwVbDxT.dpuf.

Jankowski, N. (2009) (ed.) *E-Research: Transformation in Scholarly Practice Routledge Advances in Research Methods* (London: Routledge).

Joshi, A. and Houtzager, P.P. (2012) 'Widgets or Watchdogs? Conceptual Explorations in Social Accountability', *Public Management Review*, 14:2 145–162.

Kaye, Jane, Whitley, Edgar A., Kanellopoulou, Nadja, Creese, Sadie, Hughes, Kay J. and Lund, David (2011) 'Dynamic Consent: A Solution to a Perennial Problem?' *British Medical Journal*, No. 343.

Keralis, Spencer D.C., (2012) 'Data Curation Education: A Snapshot', CLIR Publication No. 154, Council on Library and Information Resources (Washington D.C.: CLIR).

Klandermans B. (1986) 'Perceived Costs and Benefits of Participation in Union Action', *Personnel Psychology*, 39:2, 379–397.

Koninklijke Nederlandse Akademie van Wetenschappen (KNAW) (2013) *Responsible Research Data Management and the Prevention of Scientific Misconduct*. http://www.knaw.nl/en/news/publications/responsibleresearch-data-management-and-the-prevention-of-scientific-misconduct/@@download/pdf_file/20131009.pdf.

Knorr Cetina K (1999) *Epistemic Cultures. How the Sciences make Knowledge*. (Cambridge, MA: Harvard University Press).

Koch, Astrid-Christina (2014) 'Copernicus Data Policy', *Copernicus Today and Tomorrow*, Geneva, 16 January.

Korn, Naomi, and Oppenheim, Charles (2011) *Licensing Open Data: A Practical Guide*, version 2.0. http://discovery.ac.uk/files/pdf/Licensing_Open_Data_A_Practical_Guide.pdf.

Kroes, Neelie, (2011) 'Data is the New Gold', SPEECH/11/872,12th December.

Kroes, Neelie, (2013) 'The Big Data Revolution', *EIT Foundation Annual Innovation Forum*, SPEECH/13/261, Brussels, 26 March.

Kuhn, T (1962) *The Structure of scientific revolutions* (Chicago, IL: University of Chicago Press).

Kuipers, Tom and Van der Hoeven, Jeffrey (2009) *Survey results*, D3.4 PARSE.Insight,.

Lane, Robert, E. (1966) 'The Decline of Politics and Ideology in a Knowledgeable Society', *American Sociological Review*, 31:5, pp. 649–662.

Laney, D. (2001) *3-D Data Management: Controlling Data Volume*,

Velocity and Variety. http://blogs.gartner.com/doug-laney/files/2012/01/ad949-3D-Data-Management-Controlling-Data-Volume-Velocity-and-Variety.pdf.

Laur, H. (2012) 'Envisat and ERS Missions', *Advances in Atmospheric Sciences and Applications* (ATMOS) 2012, Bruges, 18–22 June.

Leonelli, S. (2014) 'Data Interpretation in the Digital Age', *Perspectives on Science*, 22:3, 397–417.

Lohr, Steve (2013) 'The Origins of 'Big Data': An Etymological Detective Story', *The New York Times*, 1 Feb. http://bits.blogs.nytimes.com/2013/02/01/the-origins-of-big-data-an-etymological-detective-story/?_r=0.

Lyon, David (2014) 'Surveillance, Snowden and Big Data: Capacities, Consequences, Critique', *Big Data & Society*, July–Dec 2014, 1–13.

Lyon, L. (2012) 'The Informatics Transform: Re-engineering Libraries for the Data Decade', *The International Journal of Digital Curation*, 7:1.

Machlup, F. (1962) *The Production and Distribution of Knowledge in the United States* (Princeton, NJ: Princeton University Press).

MacKenzie, D. and Wajcman, J. (eds) (2002) *The Social Shaping of Technology* (2nd edition) (Maidenhead: Open University Press).

Mansell, R. and Steinmuller, W.E. (2000) *Mobilizing the Information Society: Strategies for Growth and Opportunity* (Oxford: Oxford University Press).

Mansell, R, & Wehn, U (eds). (1998). *Knowledge Societies: Information Technology for Sustainable Development*. (Oxford: Published for the United Nations Commission on Science and Technology for Development by Oxford University Press).

Manyika, James, Chui, Michael, Groves, Peter, Farrell, Diana, Van Kuiken, Steve and Doshi, Elizabeth Almasi (2013) *Open Data: Unlocking Innovation and Performance with Liquid Information*, McKinsey & Company. http://www.mckinsey.com/business-functions/business-technology/our-insights/open-data-unlocking-innovation-and-performance-with-liquid-information.

Max Planck Society (2003) *Berlin Declaration on Open Access to Knowledge in the Sciences and Humanities*, http://www.zim.mpg.de/openaccess-berlin/berlin_declaration.pdf.

Mayernik, Mathew S., Callaghan, Sara, Leigh, Roland, Tedds, Jonathan, Worley, Steven, (2014) 'Peer Review of Datasets: When, Why and How', *Bulletin of the American Meteorological Society*.

McAdam, D. Tarrow, S. and Tilly. C. (2001) *The Dynamics of Contention* (New York and London: Cambridge University Press).

Melucci, A. (1988) 'Getting Involved: Identity and Mobilization in Social Movements', *International Social Movement Research* 1, 329–348.

Melucci, A. (1996) *Challenging Codes: Collective Action in the Information Age* (Cambridge: Cambridge University Press).

Merton, R. K. (1968) *Social Theory and Social Structure* (New York: Free Press).

Merton, R.K. ([1942]1973) *The Sociology of Science: Theoretical and Empirical Investigations* (Chicago, IL: University of Chicago Press).

Miller, Greg (2014) 'Autonomous Cars Will Require a Totally New Kind of Map', *Wired*. http://www.wired.com/2014/12/nokia-here-autonomous-car-maps/.

Mueller, C. (1994) 'Conflict, Networks and the Origins of Women's Liberation in Larana, E. Johnston, H. and Gusfield, J. (1994) *New Social Movements: From Ideology to identity* (Philadelphia, PA: Temple University Press) 247–248.

Nagy-Rothengass, Marta, (2014) 'Public Sector information at European Commission', *European Data Forum*. http://2014.data-forum.eu/edf2014-presentations.

National Science Board (2005) 'Long-Lived Digital Data Collections: Enabling Research and Education in the 21st Century'. http://www.nsf.gov/nsb/documents/2005/LLDDC_report.pdf.

Nativi, S., Craglia, M. and Pearlman, J. (2012) 'The Brokering Approach for Multidisciplinary Interoperability: A Position Paper', *International*

Journal of Spatial Data Infrastructures Research, 7, 1–15. http://ijsdir.jrc.ec.europa.eu/index.php/ijsdir/article/viewFile/281/319.

Networking and Information Technology R&D Program Big Data Senior Steering Group (BDSSG) (2014) 'The National Big Data R&D Initiative: Vision and Actions to be Taken'. https://www.nitrd.gov/nitrdgroups/images/0/09/Federal_BD_R&D_Thrusts_and_Priority_Themes.pdf.

Noorman, Merel, Kalaitzi, Vasso, Angelaki, Marina, Tsoukala, Victoria, Linde, Peter, Sveinsdottir, Thordis, Price, Lada and Wessels, Bridgette, (2014) *Institutional Barriers and Good Practice Solutions*, RECODE Project, Deliverable D4.1.

Nowotny, H., Scott, P. and Gibbons, M.T. (2001) *Rethinking Science: Knowledge and the Public in an Age of Uncertainty* (Cambridge: Polity Press).

Nowotny, H. Scott, P. and Gibbons M.T. (2003) 'Introduction: 'Mode 2' Revisited: The New Production of Knowledge', *Minerva* 41:3, 179–194.

Office of Management and Budget (OMB) (2013) Memorandum for the Heads of Executive Departments and Agencies: Open Data Policy-Managing Information as an Asset, M-13-13. https://www.whitehouse.gov/sites/default/files/omb/memoranda/2013/m-13-13.pdf.

Office of Science and Technology Policy (2012) 'Obama Administration Unveils "Big Data" Initiative: Announces $200 Million in New R&D Investments'. http://www.whitehouse.gov/sites/default/files/microsites/ostp/big_data_press_release.pdf.

OECD (2007) *OECD Principles and Guidelines for Access to Research Data from Public Funding* (Paris: OECD). http://www.oecd.org/science/sci-tech/oecdprinciplesandguidelinesforaccesstoresearchdatafrompublicfunding.htm.

OECD (2008) *Recommendation of the Council for Enhanced Access and More Effective Use of Public Sector Information* (Paris: OECD).

OECD (2016) 'Open Government Data'. http://www.oecd.org/gov/digital-government/open-government-data.htm.

Open Data 500 (2015) 'The OD500 Global Network', New York University. http://www.opendata500.com.

Open Data Institute (no date) 'About'. http://theodi.org/about.

Open Definition (no date) 'Conformant Licenses'. http://opendefinition.org/licenses/.

Open Knowledge Foundation (2013) 'EC Consultation on Open Research Data'. http://blog.okfn.org/2013/07/16/ec-consultation-on-open-research-data/.

Open Knowledge Foundation (2015) 'Open Definition'. http://opendefinition.org.

Open Knowledge Foundation (no date) 'What is Open?' https://okfn.org/opendata/.

PARSE.Insight Consortium (2010) *Science Data Infrastructure Roadmap*. http://www.parseinsight.eu/downloads/PARSE-Insight_D2-2_Roadmap.pdf.

Pearlman, Jay, Williams III, Albert, and Simpson, Pauline, (eds) (2013) *Report of the Research Coordination Network RCN: OceanObsNetwork. Facilitating Open Exchange of Data and Information*, NSF/Ocean Research Foundation.

Penev, Lyubomir, Mietchen, Daniel, Chavan, Vishwas, Hagedorn, Gregor, Remsen, David, Smith, Vincent, Shotton, David, (2011) *Pensoft Data Publishing Policies and Guidelines for Biodiversity Data*.

Piore, M.J. and Sabel, C. (1984) *The Second Industrial Divide: Possibilities for Prosperity* (New York: Basic Books).

Podesta J. et al. (2014) *Big Data: Seizing Opportunities Preserving Values*. (Washington D.C.: Executive Office of the President).

Polletta, F. (2004) 'Culture In and Outside Institutions', *Research in Social Movements, Conflicts, and Change*, 25, 161–183.

Pontika, N., Knoth, P. and Cancellieri, M and Pearce, S. (2015) 'Fostering Open Science to Research Using a Taxonomy and an eLearning Portal', *Proceedings of the 15th International Conference on Knowledge Technologies and Data-driven Business*, 21–22 October, Graz, Austria.

Popper, K.R. (1966) *The Open Society and Its Enemies* (5th edition, revised, 2 volumes) (Princeton, NJ: Princeton University Press).

Porat, M.U. (1977) *The Information Economy: Definition and Measurement. Vol 1.* (Washington D.C.: Department of Commerce/Office of Telecommunications).

Porter, D. (1997) *Internet Culture* (New York: Routledge).

Preece, Caroline (2015) 'Digital Catapult Partners with Data Companies to Support Data Innovation', ITPro. http://www.itpro.co.uk/strategy/24207/digital-catapult-partners-with-data-companies-to-support-data-innovation#ixzz411EVObhT.

Reichman, J.H., Uhlir, P.F. and Daederwerdere, T. (forthcoming) *Governing Digitally Integrated Genetic Resources, Data, and Literature: Global Intellectual Property Strategies for the Microbial Research Commons* (Cambridge: Cambridge University Press).

Rentier, Bernard, and Thirion, Paul. (2011) The Liège ORBi Model: Mandatory Policy without Rights Retention but Linked to Assessment Processes', *Berlin 9 Pre-conference Workshop*. http://orbi.ulg.ac.be/bitstream/2268/102031/1/Rentier-WashDC-2011.pdf.

Research and Energy (ITRE) (2013), Committee meeting -15:06 / 18:27 - 28-11-2013, record of proceedings, http://www.europarl.europa.eu/ep-live/en/committees/video?event=20131128-1500 -COMMITTEE-ITRE.

Research Councils UK (2015) 'RCUK Common Principles on Data Policy'. http://www.rcuk. ac.uk/research/datapolicy/.

Research Data Alliance (no date) 'Brokering Governance WG'. https://rd-alliance.org/groups/ brokering-governance.html.

Rheingold, H. (1993) *The Virtual Community: Homesteading on the Electronic Frontier* (Cambridge, MA: Addison-Wesley).

Ritzer, G. (1993, 2009). *The McDonaldization of Society* (Los Angeles, CA: Pine Forge Press).

Robertson, T., Döring, M, Guralnick, R., Bloom, D, Wieczorek, J, Braak, K, Otegui, H, Russell, L. and Desmet, P. (2014) 'The GBIF Integrated Publishing Toolkit: Facilitating the Efficient Publishing of Biodiversity Data on the Internet', *PLoS One*, Vol. 9:8.

Rocha, Roberto (2012) 'Anti-corruption Hackathon: An Overview', *Montreal Gazette*,12 November. http://montrealgazette.com/news/local-news/anti-corruption-hackathon-an-overview.

Roemer, R.C. and Borchardt, R. (2013) 'Institutional Altmetrics and Academic Libraries', *Information Standards Quarterly*, 25:2.

Royal Society, The (2012) 'Science as an Open Enterprise', *The Royal Society Science Policy Centre report 02/12* https://royalsociety.org/~/media/policy/projects/sape/2012-06-20-saoe.pdf.

Ruppert, E. (2015) 'Doing the Transparent State: Open Government Data as Performance Indicators', in: Rottenburg, R., Merry, S.E., Park, S-J and Mugler, J, (eds) *A World of Indicators: The Making of Governmental Knowledge through Quantification* (Cambridge, MA: Cambridge University Press), 127–150.

Science Metrix (2013) *Open Access Strategies in the European Research Area*, DG Research & Innovation, European Commission. http://www.science-metrix.com/pdf/SM_EC_OA_Policies.pdf.

Shibutani, T. (1955) 'Reference Groups as Perspectives', *American Journal of Sociology* 60: 562–569.

Soete, L. (1997) *Building the European Information Society for us all*, Final policy report of the high-level expert group (Brussels: EU-DGV).

Steinsbekk, K.S., Kåre Myskja, B. and Solberg, B. (2013) 'Broad Consent *Versus* Dynamic Consent in Biobank Research: Is Passive Participation an Ethical Problem?', *European Journal of Human Genetics*, 21, 897–902.

Staggenborg, S. (2011). *Social Movements* (Oxford: Oxford University Press).

Stainthorp, Paul (2012) An Engineering Research Data Management (RDM) Literature Review, University of Lincoln. http://orbital.blogs.lincoln.ac.uk/files/2012/04/ Literature-review.pdf.

Steele, Colin (2014) 'Open Access in Australia: National and Global Perspectives', *COASP Asia Conference*, 2–3 June, 2014 Bangkok, Thailand.

Steffen, W., Sanderson, A., Tyson, P. D., Jäger, J., Matson, P. A., Moore III, B., Oldfield, F., Richardson, K., Schellnhuber, H. J., Turner II, B. L., Wasson, R. J. (2004) *Global Change and the Earth System: A Planet under Pressure* (Berlin, Heidelberg and New York: Springer-Verlag).

Stehr, N. (2012) 'Knowledge Societies', in: Ritzer, G. (ed.) *The Wiley-Blackwell Encyclopedia of Globalization* (Cambridge: Wiley-Blackwell).

Stehr, N. (2004) 'Can the Information Society Lead to Knowledge Societies?' *Paper presented at the third session of the XXIst Century Dialogues: Building Knowledge Societies* (UNESCO/ National Commission for UNESCO of the Republic of Korea, Seoul, 27–28 July).

Stehr, N. (1994) *Knowledge Societies: The Transformation of Labour, Property and Knowledge in Contemporary Society* (London: Sage).

Stem Cell Network (2009) 'Commercialisation'. http://www.nce-rce.gc.ca/NetworksCentres-CentresReseaux/NCE-RCE/SCN-RCS_eng.asp.

Sveindottir, T., Wessels, B., Smallwood, R., Linde, P., Kala, V., Tsoukala, V. and Sondervan, J. (2013) *Stakeholder Values and Ecosystems*, RECODE D1.1. http://recodeproject.eu/wp-content/ uploads/2013/10/RECODE_D1-Stakeholder-values-and-ecosystems_Sept2013.pdf.

Swan, A. and Brown, S. (2008) *To Share or not to Share: Publication and Quality Assurance of Research Data Outputs*, (London: Research Information Network). http:// www.rin.ac.uk/our-work/data-management-and-curation/shareor-not-share-research -data-outputs.

Toulmin, S. (1972) *Human Understanding: The Collective Use and Evolution of Concepts* (Princeton, NJ: Princeton University Press).

Tsoukala, Victoria, Angelaki Marina, Kalaitzi, Vasso, Wessels, Bridgette, Price, Lada, Taylor, Mark J., Smallwood, Rod, *et al.* (2015) *Policy Guidelines for Open Access and Data Dissemination and Preservation*, RECODE Deliverable 5.1.

Turner *et al.* (2014) *The Digital Universe of Opportunities*. http://www.emc.com/leadership/ digital-universe/2014iview/internet-of-things.htm.

Tysver, Daniel. A. (2013) 'Database Legal Protection', *Bitlaw*. http://www.bitlaw.com/copyright/ database.html.

Ubaldi, B. (2013) 'Open Government Data: Towards Empirical Analysis of Open Government Data Initiatives', *OECD Working Papers on Public Governance,* No. 22, (Paris: OECD). http:// dx.doi.org/10.1787/5k46bj4f03s7-en.

UNESCO (2012) Policy Guidelines for the Development and Promotion of Open Access. (Paris: UNESCO). www.unesco.org/new/en/communication-and-information/resources/ publications-and-communication-materials/publications/full-list/towards-knowledge-societies-unesco-world-report/.

UNESCO (2005) *Towards Knowledge Societies.* (Paris: UNESCO). www.unesco.org/new/en/ communication-and-information/resources/publications-and-communication-materials/ publications/full-list/towards-knowledge-societies-unesco-world-report/.

United Nations Economic Commission for Europe (UNECE) (1998) Convention on Access to Information, Public Participation in Decision-Making and Access to Justice in Environmental Matters (a.k.a. 'Aarhus Convention') agreed at Aarhus, Denmark, on 25 June 1998.

US Chamber of Commerce Foundation (2014) *The Future of Data Driven Innovation.* https:// www.uschamberfoundation.org/sites/default/files/Data%20Report%20Final%2010.23.pdf.

University of Edinburgh (2014), 'Research Data Management Policy'. http://www.ed.ac.uk/ schools-departments/information-services/about/policies-and-regulations/research -datapolicy.

Vega-Gorgojo, Guillermo, Donovan, Anna, Finn, Rachel, Bigagli, Lorenzo, Rusitschka, Sebnem, Mestl, Thomas, Mazzetti, Paolo, *et al.* (2015) *Case Study Reports on Positive and Negative Externalities*, BYTE Project D3.2.

Vesset, D., Morris, H. D., Little, G., Borovick, L., Feldman, S., Eastwood, M. (2012) *Worldwide Big Data Technology and Services Forecast 2012–2015*, IDC http://www.idc.com/research/viewtoc. jsp?containerId=233485.

Walters, Tyler, (2009) 'Data Curation Program Development in US Universities: The Georgia Institute of Technology Example', *The International Journal of Digital Curation*, 4:3.

Webster, F. (1995) *Theories of the Information Society* (London: Routledge).

Wellcome Trust (2010) 'Policy on Data Management and Sharing'. http://www.wellcome.ac.uk/ About-us/Policy/Policy-and-position-statements/WTX035043.htm.

Wessels, B. (2010) *Understanding the Internet: A Socio-cultural Perspective* (Basingstoke: Palgrave MacMillan).

Wessels, B. (2014) *Social Change, Process and Context* (Basingstoke: Palgrave).

Wessels, B., Finn, R., Linde, P., Mazzetti, P., Nativi, S., Riley, S., Smallwood *et al.* (2014) 'Issues in the Development of Open Access to Research Data', *Prometheus Critical Studies in Innovation*, 32:2, 49–66.

The White House (2013) Executive Order – Making Open and Machine Readable the New Default for Government Information. https://www.whitehouse.gov/the-press-office/2013/05/09/ executive-order-making-open-and-machine-readable-new-default-government-.

World Wide Web Consortium (W3C) (2015) 'W3C and OGC to Collaborate to Integrate Spatial Data on the Web', Press Release, 6 January. http://www.w3.org/2015/01/spatial.html.en.

Worthy, B. (2012) 'Open Data: 'A Very Local Revolution'', *Local Government Chronicle*, 26 July.

Index